There

Is

No

ME

There

Is

No

ME

by

Jordan P. Lashley

Phase Publishing, LLC
Seattle

Cover art by Jordan P. Lashley
https://www.burningwheelyoga.com

Phase Publishing, LLC first paperback edition
March 2023

ISBN 978-1-952103-51-3
Library of Congress Control Number 2023903639
Cataloging-in-Publication Data on file.

Dedication

To all my teachers who have blazed the trail before me; because of your hard work and discipline, the path in front of me has been well worn and the lamps of knowledge that light the way are forever there to give me my bearings. For this, I am eternally grateful and in your debt.

To the students who walk the path behind me, your dedication and perseverance continually inspire me. Trust, not in me, but in all that have walked this path before me. It's not an easy road to walk, but it is well worth the effort.

To my friends who walk beside me; without your support, I would have surely fallen down long ago. Your love is what keeps me going through the darkest of times.

Dear reader,

It is my purpose with this story not so much to lay out a system of thought, in some dogmatic way, but to inspire thought. Of course, I will make certain statements, which I hope you will consider.

As you consider them, many questions may arise. If you would, please put those questions to me so that we may look at them more together, as friends do. May you be healthy. May you know peace and joy. May you realize the end of suffering. May it be a blessing.

Jordan P. Lashley

An old Cherokee is teaching his grandson about life. "A fight is going on inside me," he said to the boy. "It is a terrible fight, and it is between two wolves. One is evil—he is anger, envy, sorrow, regret, greed, arrogance, self-pity, guilt, resentment, inferiority, lies, false pride, superiority, and ego."

He continued, "The other is good— he is joy, peace, love, hope, serenity, humility, kindness, benevolence, empathy, generosity, truth, compassion, and faith. The same fight is going on inside you —and inside every other person, too."

The grandson thought about it for a minute and then asked his grandfather, "Which wolf will win?"

The old Cherokee simply replied, "The one you feed."

Introduction

Consciousness and creativity were, are, and always will be. Consciousness is the void. An infinite nothingness; a unified field of energy filled with nothing, in which the possibility for all things exists. Before there was the universe of things, there was consciousness. Conversely, creativity is the ability to create; the action of making something from the infinite nothingness. It takes creativity to reach into the void of consciousness and bring all the things into being.

Like the poles of a magnet, consciousness and creativity cannot be separated from each other. You cannot divide the positive end of a magnet from the negative. If you try to cut a magnet in half, you end up creating two magnets, each with opposing poles still intact. It is the same with consciousness and creativity, or, in the language of yogis, *shiva* and *shakti*. They are forever connected, and from them, all things come into being.

Science shows us that stars are the building blocks of the Universe. A star is formed from dust and hydrogen. Gravity swirls the dust and the hydrogen molecules together into a cloud called a nebula. The hydrogen molecules naturally repel each other, but as gravity spins the molecules faster and faster, eventually the hydrogen molecules can no longer avoid each other. They finally slam together in an explosion we call fusion. Energy is released, and a new molecule is created called helium.

While these fusion reactions are exploding outward, gravity is pulling inward at the same time. One way to observe this phenomenon would be to see these forces as fighting with each other, but this point of view in yogic terms would be an example of *avidyā*, "not seeing clearly."

In actuality, these two forces of fusion and gravity are working together to bring a star into being. The star is created when these forces come to an equilibrium, and then, for millions or billions of years, the star shines its brilliance and light into the darkness of space.

Eventually, the star will begin to run out of the hydrogen it needs to fuel the fusion, but gravity will continue to push inward, collapsing the star in on itself. In due course, the star becomes so compressed it can no longer contain itself, and finally explodes its contents in a supernova, creating a multitude of new things, or, if you will, the building blocks through which *shakti*, creativity, can make new things. At this point, gravity pushes into the empty space and becomes so dense that it creates a black hole.

From the contents of the exploding star, new things come into being, and then more things, and so on. All of the atoms and molecules that make up your body and brain came from an exploding star! In other words, that star had to die in order for you to exist. The human body and brain are so sophisticated that it can actually hold consciousness and creativity inside it; effectively making us the microcosm, or seed of the Universe. We are the embodiment of *shiva* and *shakti*.

Close your eyes and what do you see? Darkness, nothingness, an infinite void as far as you can "look" in any direction? That is consciousness. Wait a bit, and you begin to see color and form shifting and morphing, very similar to the nebulas in space I was just talking about. When you look at an image of a nebula, it's almost like you can see the "finger" of creativity reaching into the void and swirling up the gravity to bring a star into being.

In the same way, everything that humankind has brought into being, from telescopes and airplanes to smart phones, nuclear bombs, and even YOU, were all brought into being in the same way. Close your eyes and reach into the void of *shiva*. The possibility for any "thing" is there. With *shakti*, you pull it into being.

My creation story, just like any other human, is actually a continuation of someone else's story. None of us is separate, or individual. All of our stories are woven together in a beautiful tapestry of cause and effect, but as humans, we often feel separate and experience duality.

You are somewhere reading this right now. I am somewhere writing this at some other time. Maybe we have never even met. This is an example of the experience of the duality; self and other. "I am here, and you are there." However, if you close your eyes and become still, you can experience the oneness I am talking about. There is only oneness. There is only consciousness. You are not a "part" of it. You are it, and so am I.

If I asked you to tell me who "you" are, what would you tell me? You might start with your name and how many laps you have completed around the sun. Perhaps you would then tell me whether or not you were married, how many children you had, and what you do for work. But yogis and neurobiologists agree that what you think of as "you" is just a story, and that story is just a collection of memories in your brain of what consciousness has experienced through the senses of the form you call your "self." But is that who you really are? Don't you feel that there is so much more to who and what you are, and that for some reason, it's hard to put the rest of it into words?

Even the content of your brain is not entirely your own. It has the content of every brain that has come before yours. We download it into each other through education, culture, society, and tradition. The experience of individuality seems real, but if one goes a little deeper, one sees it is an illusion.

Think of the ocean. When a wave comes into being, it is formed from the ocean, but it has its own shape and size, and for a while has its own existence, until it breaks and crashes back into the whole ocean. Was the wave ever actually an individual? If you put your big toe in the ocean, doesn't the whole of your body know the water is wet, and whether it is warm or cold? So too, everything you experience, consciousness experiences. What one human does affects us all.

Still don't believe me? Let's say I ask you to look at the moon. I say, "Look at the moon," and without looking, you say, "I don't see it." What I am asking you to do is *look*. It is there. Look for yourself, and you will see it. It doesn't have anything to do with belief. It just *is*.

We all have things about life that we wish were different. We might make up a belief that things *are* the way we wish they were, but that doesn't change things and only leads us to suffering. Yoga is about radically accepting things as they are. What is, is. Whether we like it or not does not matter. It still is.

Maybe we know each other and maybe we don't, but I bet that I could ask some questions, and we would answer them in the same way. We would answer them the same way because we are the same consciousness. We are two waves in the same ocean, two toes on the same foot.

Do you want to be happy? Me too. Do you experience pain and loneliness? Me too. Do you want to suffer? Me neither. I could keep going, but I think you get the point. I could ask those same questions to anyone, anywhere on the planet, at any time, regardless of race, social standing, and circumstance, and we would all answer them the same way. So maybe we have never met, but I know you and you know me. The Truth is that there has only, ever, been *us*.

Chapter One

I entered into what we call life, or existence, on July the 1st, 1979. I left the safety and security of my incubation inside my mother and entered the cold, harsh reality of life. As the saying goes, "We enter the world cold, hungry, and crying, and then it gets worse!" Well, like most human newborns, I am sure I was sticky, slimy, and crying.

As my parents tell the tale, my mother knew she was going into labor, so she and my father went to the hospital only to be sent home by the doctor who said she was not ready. My mother was sure it was time. I was her third child, so instead, they went to a nearby Denny's restaurant, the only thing open in the wee hours of the morning.

Eventually, my mother's water broke, or something else definitive enough, and they were admitted to the hospital. It was a relatively easy birth as far as these things can be. The doctor held me up and announced, "You have a beautiful baby boy!" At which point, I promptly shit all over him. My parents always say, "We knew right there and then that you would be trouble."

I was the delightful "surprise" child to Betty Crocker and Hank Hill. I'm just kidding, but not really. My parents always wanted the quintessential 1950s, Americana, nuclear family, and they had it—complete with poodle skirts, sock hops, potluck dinners, and church on Sundays. Mom stayed home to take care of us kids, clean the house to museum standards, and cook delicious meals crafted from ingredients that came from a box, a can, or the freezer. Meanwhile, dad worked his way up the corporate ladder selling computers to make the money necessary for retirement, college for us kids, and safety and security for us all.

It is a noble aspiration to provide and care for those you love. My parent's plan has served them well their entire lives, and they have lived together happily for over fifty years now. We always had food on the table, a roof over our heads, nice clothes, education, two cars in the garage, a big TV, and nice vacations in the summer. We never wanted for anything.

For me, however, it always felt empty, a little hollow, and kind of superficial, and I found myself asking the question, "Is this what life is really all about?" I always felt like there was something deeper that I was missing.

I really don't want to come off as if I am hating on my parents here, so let me be clear. They have always loved me unconditionally, cared for me exceptionally, and I love them both dearly. It's just that their model for happiness has never really worked for me, and I had a hard time figuring out why.

Going back as far as eight years old, I remember saying things like, "I don't want to be here!" I was not referring to being with my parents or my family, but rather, being in this *life*. I would say, "I didn't ask to be brought into this existence. This was my parents' decision, and now I have to live with it."

When I think back on this now, it's kind of an unusual thing for an eight-year-old to say. My daughter is eleven now, and I can't even imagine how I would respond to a statement like that from her.

When I was born, we lived in a small town outside of Pittsburgh, Pennsylvania. I don't know how much of these early years I actually remember. I do know all the stories that my family tells about me when we gather around the dinner table at the holidays; like the one about me on the first day of preschool at the Methodist church. I was sent to the principal's office for saying to the teacher, "Your boobies are much bigger than my Mommy's." According to my father, this was not an inaccurate assessment.

Another time, a few months later, my mother was sick and had taken some cold medicine that made her drowsy. Apparently, she fell asleep, and when she didn't arrive to pick me up at school, I decided to walk home. About a mile down the road, the principal caught up with me in his car, frazzled and sort of panicking.

He asked, "What do you think you're doing?" I said, "Walking home. I know where it is." He said, "I don't care if you know where it is. Get in the car!"

My mom says I broke her heart on the first day of kindergarten when she attempted to walk me to the school bus. I stopped her at the front door, put my hand on her and said, "I'm good, Mommy. I've got this."

The image of the independent, free speaking, black sheep that gets painted of me in these stories became *my* story. It became my reality. It is, was, and always will be, to some extent, how I see myself. I did these things, after all, so they must say something about who I am, right? How is it that someone else's stories about me influence the way I see myself? Doesn't that seem silly? But we all do it. We think that the content of our brains is entirely our own, but it is not.

I have memories blessed to me from being born in a digital age; you know, those moments that are eternally captured in photographic or video form. My father first had a 35mm, Super 8, reel-to-reel video recorder with no sound. Then, in the 80s, he bought a personal camcorder. He loved to capture the family on VHS tapes, and he still goes back and watches them often, reveling in the memories.

My daughter's first nine years of life are documented in surprising detail in my Facebook memories, which is odd to think about. Facebook was brand new when she was born, and we were all fascinated by it, but I have become disenchanted with it. In the beginning, it seemed as though Facebook was bringing us all together. It was like having all my friends in my pocket. But now, it just seems to be driving us all apart. There are lots of good things that have come from social media, but now, twenty years into it, I think the harm far outweighs the benefits.

In one of my father's videos, my sister is performing her dance recital routine in the kitchen while I am standing in the background picking my nose. I don't remember actually doing this. I just have the memory of watching the video. I even have "memories" of things that happened before I was born. I have a grainy 35mm memory of my mother attempting to fly a kite; running, tripping, and falling flat on her face. It's the oldest "fail" video I've ever seen.

My first real memory is something entirely different.

It's not a video, or a picture, or even an image in my brain. It is more visceral than that, more sensory. It's the feeling of being warm, content, and rocking gently. In this memory, it is very bright, like when the sun comes through your eyelids, and someone is humming softly. This memory is more real and tangible to me than any of the aforementioned stories. Why? Because they are just stories. This memory was imprinted in my brain by my senses. It was so "pleasant" that it stuck.

I have another memory from this time that stuck for a different reason. I must have been about five years old, because we were still living in Pennsylvania, and we moved to Massachusetts when I was going into first grade.

We had a swimming pool, and the rule was that no one was allowed in the house with a wet bathing suit. My usual modus operandi was to strip off my bathing suit at the door to the house when I was finished swimming and run up to my room naked.

This was all well and good until my sister, who was five years older than me, had a group of friends over to swim. You know what happened don't you?

We were all swimming, playing, and generally having a good time, and then we decided to go inside. We got to the door, and I stripped off my suit to the sound of my sister exclaiming, "Jordan! No! What are you doing?" I was thinking, "What I always do, no trunks in the house." They pointed and laughed, but I had no idea what I had done wrong.

This was the first time I ever experienced embarrassment. Even as I was writing this book, I found myself wanting to avoid this memory. I chose to preoccupy myself with washing dishes and laundry so I wouldn't have to relive it. This memory was so "painful" that it stuck.

My point is that memory is subjective. Some of them you actually own, others were given to you, and others are preserved for the ages in digital form. Upon every one of those memories, the Ego, which is our sense of self, identifies with things and experiences as it imprints each memory into our brains and labels them "pleasurable" or "painful."

All the stories and events that I share here are only how I remember them and are therefore all biased and incomplete to some degree. I mention other people only as necessary to their role in my story, and I change their names for privacy. I promise to write my truth, knowing that it is also my fiction. It may not align with how other people remember these events. I can't speak to their truth. This is how I remember it; how it is embedded in me. These are the things I have learned from the events in my life so far as I search for balance.

Neurologists say that every time we remember something, our brains reprocess the information. If the memory is labeled "pleasurable", we will enhance the details that we enjoyed. If the memory is labeled "painful," we will enhance the parts that hurt us. But we don't realize we are doing this consciously, do we? We treat it as if it were an instant replay from a sporting event. We believe that we have gone into the memory and analyzed it, and that now it is more accurate than the original event.

But of course, it's not. It is flawed, incomplete, and distorted. Three people involved in the same situation will all remember it their own way, and that will be their subjective truth.

What is yoga philosophy? Well, the word philosophy comes from the ancient Greeks and means, "for the love of wisdom". In yoga philosophy, we are after objective Truth; the ability to see things as they actually are, without memory, preference, or beliefs attached. We are seeking *vidyā*, "to see what is."

People often take the meaning of philosophy to be theoretical, and while yoga definitely has its theistic realms, I, like the Buddha, am more interested in what we can know now. He was, after all, a yogi, an ascetic. He broke from tradition in the sense that he wanted humans to focus on living the best quality life *right now*. If we live our best life right now, then the whole theory of karma and transmigration is kind of moot.

Most Westerners think of yoga as exercise or a good stretch. The *asānas*, or postures, are what have become the most popular, but they are only one aspect of the yoga practice. Another misconception is that yoga is about longevity, and that if you practice yoga, you will be guaranteed a long life. The postures will certainly keep the body healthy, strong, and stress free, if that is your karma, but the True goal of yoga is liberation from suffering. It is not about longevity, because none of us has ultimate influence over that, although we may believe we do.

We like to convince ourselves that if we eat the right food and exercise enough and don't smoke or drink that we will guarantee ourselves a long life. But that simply isn't True, that is a belief. What's True is that you may never smoke a cigarette and still die of lung cancer. You might be the healthiest person in the world and still get hit by a car.

We don't know what will take us out in the end, but something will. Yoga is really about quality of life; living the best quality of life we can. Why worry about the things we can't control, when we can focus on the things we can?

Chapter Two

The Theory of Transmigration, more commonly known as reincarnation, goes something like this…

The soul goes through many lives. It starts its first life as an amoeba, and then evolves into more and more complex animals with each life, learning and growing in awareness with every cycle. Eventually, the soul makes it to a human life where it develops an Ego and experiences duality. Not understanding the principle of karma or cause and effect, human souls at first live selfish lives.

If someone were to punch you in the face in this life, your automatic response would probably be to punch them right back without thought of consequence. It would be a primitive response, like that of a wild animal. A wild animal responds to violence with violence, and love with love. As your soul lives through many unaware human lives like this, the conditions of each life become more unpleasant and unfortunate as all the karma plays itself out.

What makes humans change and respond to violence with love instead? Mindfulness. What is mindfulness? Mindfulness is time. Time which ends up feeling like space in the mind. This space, or time, is between stimulus and response; stimulus being information coming from the senses. Mindfulness is taking a moment to pause and reflect upon the stimulus and then choosing a way to respond. The opposite of mindfulness would be stimulus and then reaction. Reaction is a repeated action; doing the things you always do without reflection.

Having repeated the unmindful pattern of action so many times, for so many lives, we finally get to a life where we decide to choose differently. Someone hits us in the face, but this time, having evolved past our basic animal instincts, we decide to respond not with violence, but with compassion and kindness. According to the theory, the reward for a mindful life is a life of virtue, that is to say, now your purpose is to show others how to evolve above and beyond their base nature. It takes living a life of virtue to be given a fortunate human birth.

What is a fortunate human birth? Well, in the old days, it meant that you were born a prince, who became a king, who had the power and resources to affect great change. In this day and age, it means something a little different. Nowadays, it may mean being born into a religious family who gets you thinking about spiritual matters from an early age, or it could also mean being born into a family that has the resources to educate and care for you. If you were given food, shelter, education and love, consider yourself fortunate, because not everyone gets that.

For all purposes, I have had a fortunate human life. I have not known death, disease, or catastrophe in any major way. I have been loved, cared for, and educated. How do most people who have had every opportunity in life handed to them on a silver platter behave? Mindful? Virtuous? No, not really, right? They act pretty selfishly, don't they?

According to the Transmigration Theory, if we live a

fortunate life in this way, then we have missed the whole point, and we are sent back to the beginning, to start the process all over again. However, if we arrive in a fortunate life and live it with mindfulness and virtue, at our death, we are given options. We are able to choose to transcend birth and death, and move into the celestial realms, or return to a human life to help others escape *saṃsāra*, the wheel of birth and death. Those who choose to return are what's known as *bodhisattvas*. *Bodhi* means intellect, and *sattva* means purity and tranquility. A *bodhisattva* is someone who has cultivated an intellect of purity and tranquility.

The Transmigration Theory is a good theory. It's my favorite one, but it is still just a theory. Who knows if it's True? Maybe we will find out in death, or maybe we won't. You can see why, if we just concern ourselves with living our best life, then we won't incur the karma. We will be mindful and virtuous naturally, and so the whole thing is moot. Death is an inevitability that we have no control over and that no one really understands.

Oh, sure, people will tell you they know, but they don't. How could they? Don't waste your life concerned about what happens when you die. Focus on how you can live the highest quality of life that is free from suffering right now. Focus on the present.

My mother and her parents are and were very religious people. They are Christians; not Catholics, but Protestants. My mother would be fine with the term Born Again

Christian. The town where I group up was very
conservative and very Christian, and for the first six years
of my life, God, Jesus, the Devil, and the Holy Spirit were
all things that were talked about in daily conversation, as
easily as discussing the weather. All of it was generally
accepted, not as beliefs, but as Truth.

When I was entering the first grade, my father decided
to take a promotion at work, which meant we would be
moving to Massachusetts. I wasn't nervous or scared about
the move; I was more excited for the new adventure. My
older sister was going into junior high, and my older brother
was headed to high school, and they were not as thrilled.

As I began primary school, two things became
apparent fairly quickly. First, I talked funny (I had a strange
accent), and because of this, I felt the need to change the
way I spoke. And second, I noticed that people in
Massachusetts were of a very different mindset. They
responded differently when Jesus or the Devil was
mentioned.

I would label the difference as liberal and scientific
versus my conservative and religious roots. Although I
could not have articulated that in this way at the time, I liked
it, and worked hard to integrate and make friends. And my
hard work paid off. I made good friends and received solid
marks on my schoolwork. But I was a bit of a troublemaker.

I can best describe myself in grades one through five
as Bart Simpson. I was intelligent and got bored quickly and
would act out to entertain myself. I loved to make people
laugh, which drove my teachers crazy, and I spent many
recesses inside, while my friends were outside playing. My
teacher would make me stay in and write the definition of

self-control over and over again as punishment. Still to this day, I can recite Webster's Dictionary definition of self-control verbatim. "Self-discipline means careful control and training of oneself."

The meaning of these words was lost on me at the time. I just saw it as a punishment to complete, as fast as I could, so I could go outside and play. The teacher would always give me a specific number of times that I had to write it, but as I said, I was smart. I figured out that if I wrote one word at a time, it went way faster. I would write "self" twenty-five times, and then "discipline" twenty-five times, and so on. The irony is that I was using self-discipline to get it done faster.

I was always being sent to the principal's office, and now I understand why. My teachers would inevitably become frustrated with the rambunctious kid who loved to push their buttons, and off to the dreaded principal's office I would go. I was sent there so often that after a while it didn't even scare me anymore. I became used to it, desensitized.

One day, I was sent down there, but the principal was busy, so his secretary told me to sit and wait. As I was sitting there bored, I reached into my pocket and found a twisty tie that I had taken off something in my lunch earlier in the day. You know what a twisty tie is, right? It's a length of wire about three inches long covered in plastic that you use to hold the top of a plastic bag closed.

The first thing I did was use my teeth to pull all the plastic off of the wire. That occupied me for a while. Then I started playing with the wire, tapping it on things. There was a light switch on the wall next to me, and without thinking about what I was doing, I began to trace the wire around the switch. I don't know if I stuck it in there on purpose or if somehow it just slipped in, but without warning, a three-foot-long bolt of blue-white light shot out of the wall, and I jumped back in my chair.

Thankfully, I was not electrocuted, but it scared the hell out of me. At that moment, the power went out in the office. I stuck my head out the door and clunk, another block of lights went out in the hallway! Clunk, another. Clunk, another. I watched every circuit breaker in the school blow one at a time in horror. I thought, "I'm already in trouble. Now I am in *so* much trouble."

The secretary, who was also shocked and horrified said, "You're lucky you're not dead." The principal called my mom and made her come pick me up, and I remember him saying to her, "Just take him home. I don't even know what to do with him!"

I dreaded parent-teacher conferences and letters home from school. At the start of each new year, the teacher would say something like, "Oh, you're Jordan. I've been warned about you." But whenever I received my report card, I always had straight A's. I didn't think anything of it. I assumed everyone did.

Here's the thing. I wasn't trying to cause problems. I didn't enjoy getting in trouble. I didn't want my parents to be angry with me. I was just being myself, but for years, being me got me into a lot of trouble. I was labeled a problem child and a troublemaker. But like I said, I wasn't trying to be bad.

After years of this, I started to believe all the things people were saying about me. I finally said to myself, "Fine!

If everyone thinks I'm bad, I must be. I am going to show them all just how bad I can be!" And then, right around this time, it happened; an event from which there would be no turning back, an event that would further fuel my anger so much so that by the time I arrived in middle school, I loved the phrase, "I'm pissed off, and the whole world owes me."

Until the age of eight, I was a Christian. I believed that Jesus had died for our sins, that God the Father lived in heaven, and that the Holy Spirit lived in me. I had been taught that God loved me, and wanted me to be happy, and I believed. I believed it fervently, if an eight-year-old could be fervent about anything. I defended my faith strongly and was often ridiculed for it.

Nintendo's first entertainment system had just come out, and I had received one for Christmas. To say that I was obsessed with Super Mario Bros.® would have been an understatement. I played that game until I had blisters on my thumbs in the shape of the buttons and D-pad.

This particular day, my friend came over and brought some of his game cartridges with him. We started playing, and then my friend died in the game and yelled out, "Oh, God damn it!" I was shocked and offended. I told him, "You can't say that! Please apologize. It's a sin to take God's name in vain." When he refused to apologize, I popped out his game and asked him to leave.

See what I mean? I was pretty fanatical for a little kid. These exchanges happened fairly often, and people acted like I was crazy; like I believed unicorns were real.

Fast forward to third grade. It was just before Christmas, and I was on the school bus on the way home from school, and I made some comment about how I was excited for Santa Claus to come. I have such a vivid image in my head of my friend peeking over the back of the seat with a look of pity on his face.

He said, "You don't still believe in Santa, do you?"

"What do you mean?" I replied.

"Santa isn't real," he said. "It's your parents, man. It's your parents who put the presents under the tree," and then he laughed like I was an idiot.

I looked at my friends, and they all seemed to agree with him. So what did I do? I defended my belief in Santa the same way I had often defended my belief in God. I got angry.

"You're wrong! My parents wouldn't lie to me!" I exclaimed.

I ran home, convinced that my mom would tell me that Santa was real, and that they were wrong. When I told her, I did not get the reaction I was expecting. My mother paused, bit her bottom lip, and my heart sank. She said, "Well, I guess you are old enough now to know the truth. Santa isn't real."

To say that I was devastated doesn't begin to describe it. I know, you are probably laughing right now. I get it. Finding out that Santa is not real is not very traumatic for most children, but in that moment when my mother uttered those three words, everything changed.

I cautiously asked my mother, "What else have you and Dad lied to me about?"

"Well," she said, "the Tooth Fairy and the Easter Bunny aren't real, either."

My heart sank a little more. "Why would my parents lie to me about this?" I thought, "Were they laughing at me behind my back? Did they think I was stupid?"

Most children might have made the connection between Santa and maybe the Easter Bunny or the Tooth Fairy, but I took it a step further. You see, in my eight-year-old brain, Santa was an old man with a big white beard whom I couldn't see, but who somehow managed to watch me all the time and judge everything I did. If I was good, and did what he wanted me to do, I was rewarded with presents once a year.

God was also an old man with a big white beard who I couldn't see who watched and judged everything I did. If I was good and did everything God wanted me to do, I was rewarded with Heaven at the end of my life. It didn't seem like too far of a jump to me.

In the Vedic tradition in India, members of the priest caste are known as Brahman. Young Brahman boys begin their spiritual life at the age of eight. The logic behind this is that prior to then, because their brains are still forming, children don't know the difference between right and wrong. After the age of eight, children may still take wrong action, but by then, they have enough awareness to know it is wrong. I had quite the opposite experience, as you can see. I was eight years old, and instead of just beginning, my spiritual life, it seemed, had come to an end.

I know it shouldn't have been that big of a deal, but it was for me. It is not lost on me that the most traumatic thing that ever happened during my childhood was finding out that Santa wasn't real. In comparison with the loss of a parent, or being born into poverty, or any of the other horrible things children go through all the time, it's laughable.

It's okay. Laugh. I laugh about it now, too. I know now that my parents meant no harm, but at the time, those three words, "Santa isn't real", destroyed my trust in my family, my connection with the divine, and affected every decision I would make for the next fifteen years.

Shortly after this, I remember asking someone, I wish I could remember who, "What do you call a person who doesn't believe in God?"

I was told, "An atheist." I thought, "Okay, I'm not a Christian. I'm an atheist. I'm an atheist, and I'm trouble, got it? Watch out world, here I come!"

Chapter Three

My dear wife, Angela, is the love of my life. She is the best partner and friend I could ask for, but music has always been my mistress. My love affair with music has kept me going at several points in my life when I didn't want to keep going, and it began with my grandfather, Pop. That is what my brother, sister, and I called him. My cousins, who were older than us, called him Pap. When my brother was little, he would try to say Pap, but it came out Pop, and it stuck. I think Pop suited him better, anyway.

Pop was five feet tall, had a big, round belly, and had been a test pilot in World War II. He was a musician and had a big-band jazz band. With his fedora, goatee, and horn-rimmed glasses, he was one hip cat. He had the kindest eyes, and boy, did he love me. He loved to dote on me and was very generous with his time and attention.

When I was four or five, he gave me my first saxophone lesson. The saxophone was too large for me to hold, so he would put it in its stand so I could play it that way. He taught me to curl my bottom lip over my teeth, place my top teeth on top of the mouth piece, squeeze the mouthpiece gently with my lips, and blow. Squawk! If you have never had the pleasure of hearing the saxophone played with absolutely no skill by a five-year-old, let me tell you it is a particularly horrible sound, very shrill and squeaky.

But my grandfather didn't care. He would smile from ear to ear and clap like it was the most beautiful melody he had ever heard. This was the beginning, and since then, music has been a refuge for my soul. The vibrations transport me into emotional spaces that light me up when I am dim, hold me when I am sad and lonely, and always seem to express that which I can't seem to find words for.

I would spend hours and hours in my room sitting and reading the liner notes from the most recent album I had saved up to buy. That's right, kids. This was pre-Spotify. This was back in the days when your only music choices were whatever the radio was playing or your own album collection. We didn't have access to every song ever recorded at the tips of our fingers. I would read the lyrics on the album cover over and over until I had them memorized and could sing along. It was the 80s, and rock was king. Guns & Roses, Motley Crue, and Ozzy Ozborne were some of my faves.

In my teen years, I got a subscription to BMG music, which sent a new album of my choosing to my door every month. This is how I got my introduction to classic rock like The Doors, Led Zeppelin, and Cream. In the 90s, it was all about grunge, flannel shirts and Doc Martens, and the sounds of Alice in Chains, Soundgarden, and Pearl Jam. All this music, all these sounds, vibrations, and waves in different forms had deep influences on me.

Scientists say that the Universe began with a bang. The Bible says, "In the beginning, there was the word, and the word was with God, and the word was God". A bang and a word are both sounds, vibrations, waves. In yoga, it is actually the vowel sounds of the Sanskrit alphabet that are the creation myth, which goes like this...

Shiva (consciousness) was an energy, an energy in wave form. If there had been an ear to hear this energy at the time, it would have sounded like "a." *Shakti's* (creativity's) vibration also sounded like an "a," because *shiva* and *shakti* are one and the same. When combined, they sound like a long "ah" sound; think of angels singing. That is why it is such a divine sound when the choir sings "ah," because it is the sound of the primordial vibration.

Shiva and *shakti* increased their energy until the "ah" sound became "i," pronounced "e", and then "ī," pronounced "ee." As it began to increase in power, the sound became "u" and "ū," still building to "e," "ai," "o," and "au," until they took all the power and condensed it into a single point, "aṃ."

Finally, with the sound of "ah," pronounced "aha," the Universe exploded into being. What we are talking about here is energy, and energy is a wave, and a wave has a peak and a trough. The distance from the peak, through the trough, to the next peak is how we measure energy.

If we are measuring sound, we use the Hertz scale. In the visual light spectrum, we call it Kelvin. When you shorten the wave, the pitch goes up. As *shiva* and *shakti* increased their energy, the pitch changed, thus the different sounds. The sound of the creation of the Universe is Om-Aha. When we chant "om," we are making the sound of the vibration that brought the Universe into being. The "aha" is the sound of the big bang.

Now, consider those moments in life when you have

had an epiphany, a stroke of insight. What sound do you typically associate with insight? "Aha!", isn't it? And when you have an "aha" moment, doesn't it feel like a Universe of understanding just exploded into being in your brain? Where does insight come from? Is it a product of thought? Or is it something else entirely?

Well, wherever the insight had come from, I had clearly come to a point of change. Certain experiences had occurred, and I had arrived at some conclusions. I was angry, alone, and hurt, and I translated that outwardly into a persona of someone who didn't care. I did everything I was told *not* to do by society, religion, and authority, and thought, "Fuck you! No one is going to tell me how to live my life!"

I looked to my MTV heroes and decided that I needed to be a rocker. I was going to live hard and fast, and hopefully die young and leave a good-looking corpse. In seventh-grade science, we were taught the dangers of smoking cigarettes, and I decided it was a good time for me to start smoking. After all, it would take ten to twelve years off my life that I didn't want anyway.

My father had quit smoking when I was born. He said he had two images in his mind that he used to quit. The first was a picture of a man smoking with the cigarette attached to the end of his tracheotomy tube. My dad put that picture on the bathroom mirror, so that he was forced to see it every morning. The second thing that inspired him to quit was the image in his mind of being able to run up a hill with me.

These were the tools he used to conquer his cravings; one positive and one negative. He was essentially asking his ego which future it wanted to attach to. One day, he purchased his final pack of cigarettes and placed them in the top drawer of his dresser where they sat and waited for thirteen years. Ironically, his last pack of cigarettes became my first pack of cigarettes.

My first cigarette made me choke and cough just like anyone else, but I was determined to get it right, plus, when I stopped coughing, I felt lightheaded and dizzy and pretty good. I loved the way other kids would react to my smoking. They told us not to smoke, and I was smoking.

Now I was really getting somewhere. My parents still restricted my clothing and hairstyle, but now I had something to show everyone that I was breaking the rules.

You might be wondering how a thirteen-year-old was getting cigarettes. Well, back then, they weren't as strict with the 18+ law. We would just stand outside the store and ask people who were walking in to buy them for us. We would offer to buy their pack.

That would work sometimes, but the best way to get them was to sneak out of the house at night. I would wait until after midnight and walk to the twenty-four-hour convenience store with my friends. I'm not sure why, but at two in the morning, no one seemed to have a problem selling us cigarettes.

One night, after we had bought our cigarettes, the police rolled up on us when we were walking back home.

My friend said, "Yo, 5-0 behind us! What should we do?"

"Just keep walking, maybe he won't stop us," I said.

No such luck. I heard from behind me, "Hey! Stop! Where are you going?" the police officer yelled.

Apparently, they had received complaints about someone setting off fireworks nearby. He asked, "Do you boys know anything about that?" We said, "No." And then he made us empty our pockets.

He confiscated our cigarettes, and when my friend pulled out a string of fireworks, that was it. We were done. The cop called our parents and drove us home. My parents were less than pleased to be woken up by the police at two a.m. to be told about my involvement with cigarettes and fireworks. I was busted. But I didn't quit. I took whatever punishment they gave me and kept right on doing what I was doing.

A few of my friends had started smoking marijuana. They smoked it around me several times, but I didn't have any interest. I was good with my cigarettes. One day, it was my friend's birthday, and he said, "Come on, man! Smoke with me. It's my birthday." So I said, "Fine. Give it to me." And I was immediately in love.

I have smoked marijuana pretty much every day since. The only reasons I haven't are because of lack of funds or availability. Not what you were expecting me to say? Yeah, I'm not going to get all public service announcement-y on you. That is not this book. Don't expect me to get all "Drugs are bad, m-kay," because I don't think drugs are bad, and I don't regret anything I have done. I am grateful for all the positive and negative experiences I have had. The positive and the negative are not fighting each other. They are working together to make me who I am, like fusion and gravity working together to make a star.

With a few of my friends from the school jazz band, I started my first rock band in eighth grade. We had guitar,

29

bass, drums, and I was the singer. We were all quite talented for our age.

First, we called ourselves South of Heaven, after the Slayer song, because the guitarist was a metal head. But that wasn't my vision for the band, and when he quit, I made the decision to teach myself to play the guitar.

Slimmed down to a three-piece punk band, we re-named ourselves Outpatience; like outpatients from a hospital but spelled like "out of patience." We thought we were so clever.

My parents were always supportive of whatever I was interested in. I tried every sport, Cub Scouts, Indian Guides, but nothing seemed to hold my interest. At some point, one of my schoolteachers noticed some artistic ability in me, and I received private art lessons in drawing and painting, which I did for a little while. But my band was everything.

One day, I was rehearsing my latest song, which meant I was wailing on my guitar and screaming more or less, when my father burst into the room. I believe I had said a swear which was what set him off. He made it very clear that if this was what I was doing with these friends of mine, he was not going to let me do it anymore.

At the time, the band was the only thing keeping me alive. It felt like all I had. I looked my father in the eye and said, "If you take this away from me, I will never forgive you." He must have seen the seriousness in my face. He heard me, and asked, "What are you so angry about?"

I didn't know. I didn't have the self-knowledge to understand that yet. All I knew was that I was very, very angry at everything, and all the testosterone didn't help. I wasn't very excited about being alive. I wouldn't say I was suicidal, but I definitely considered it. Suicide was a way out, but outrightly killing myself seemed like a defeat. Living recklessly and maybe expediting my death in the process? That seemed to make more sense.

Alan Watts says that the only real philosophical question worth asking is whether or not to kill yourself, and at thirteen, I was already asking it. Here's the thing. Something in me still knew that life had a purpose, in spite of all its hardships and suffering. Maybe that was just it.

If there was a purpose to this life, then there must be a purpose to all the suffering, to getting through the suffering. If I was supposed to go through it all, there must be the possibility that if I cut out early at my own hand, I would have to go through it all again! The risk was too high. So I made a decision. I wasn't going to outright shoot myself, but if it happened early because of some dangerous living, that was okay by me.

Chapter Four

For my freshman year of high school, we moved to a new town about forty-five minutes away. I'd had the same group of friends since first grade, and, just as I was about to enter high school, my dad decided it was time to downsize. My brother and sister were both off at college, and from his point of view, it made sense, but from my point of view, it sucked.

I attended the public school in the new town and didn't really click with anyone. I missed my friends terribly. I spent most of freshman year waiting for the weekend to come so I could go back to my hometown. I hated gym class and being forced to shower at school, so I skipped nine consecutive Mondays in a row so I wouldn't have to go.

Eventually, I was figured out, and my parents were at their wits end with me. Even though I hadn't believed in God for years, they were still forcing me to attend church every Sunday morning, and then to return in the evenings for Youth Group, where I had a few decent friends who attended a private Christian school a few towns away. I don't know, I guess I was tired of getting in trouble and getting punished.

I decided to try and clean up my act. I changed my clothes, cut my hair, quit my band, and convinced my parents to send me to the Christian school. I thought I could fake it. I thought I could be the person that Christianity and my parents said I should be. I wasn't happy with what I was doing, so I thought I would give it one more try.

I tried to make it work, I really did, but I just felt like a fraud. In Bible study classes, I would see all these holes in the doctrine, and I would ask questions that made the teachers uncomfortable. I would get answers like, "You shouldn't ask such things," and, "You need to have faith and trust God." I found these answers frustrating.

The teacher told my parents, "Jordan has a keen intellect and insight into the scriptures, but it's as though he's always trying to prove it wrong." I wasn't really. I was trying to understand. I didn't like that it didn't hold up to my questioning. I wanted a philosophy that wasn't flawed, that didn't have giant holes and leaps of faith. I wanted Truth.

J. Krishnamurti is famous for saying that "Truth is a pathless land. No religion, no guru, no nation, no authority can lead you to the Truth." Unfortunately, I didn't find Krishnamurti until much later. At this point, I was surrounded by people at home, at school, and at church who were once again telling me that I was wrong for being me, and for thinking the things I thought.

Once again, I was having suicidal thoughts. I just wanted to give up. This went on for months, and eventually I had an insight. It occurred to me that if the Christian God is who the Bible says he is, then questioning him should not make me suicidal. "Every time I try this path, it makes me depressed," I thought.

So I finally decided I was done with religion for good. And this time, I meant it. Christianity was not making me happy and whole, and it would not be my path to Truth. So what did I do? Well, I returned to my troublemaking ways of course!

I started dating the daughter of the Christian school secretary. I took her to see a Violent Femmes concert with a couple of friends, and during the concert, my girlfriend and I took turns going to the bathroom to smoke pot.

My girlfriend's friend was not happy about that, and, after the concert, she told my girlfriend's mom. Her mom called my mom, and well, that was the end of my days at the Christian school. My parents were not going to pay for me to go to private school and pull all the same shit when I could do it at public school for free.

My older brother was living in Nashville, TN at this time, and he suggested to my parents that maybe it would be good for me to go live with him for the summer. I don't know why my parents thought this was a good idea, except that maybe we all needed a break from each other. He was eight years older than me, and I certainly wanted to go. I desperately wanted freedom from my parents.

I should probably mention that my brother and I had never been close. He had pretty much tortured me my entire childhood. Oh no? You don't believe me? He used to do things like give me a wedgie and then hang me on a doorknob. Since my feet couldn't touch the ground, I would be forced to hang there until someone came and found me, or my underwear ripped enough.

One time, he tricked me into licking a plantar wart on his foot by asking me to have a contest to see who could stick out their tongue for the longest. Another time, he tied me to the side of his bureau with the bottom drawer open, and when I struggled to get free, I fell over and clothes lined my throat on the bottom drawer. He told me to wear a turtleneck so he wouldn't get into trouble! Do I need to keep going? I think you get the idea.

He left for college when I was ten years old. We went to visit him once, and he suggested that I stay with him in his dorm room. My older brother wanted to hang out with me! I was so excited, but he ended up going to a party, and I ended up in the hotel room with my parents. I was crushed. Nothing ever seemed to work out with my brother and me.

In spite of it all, though, I still looked up to him, the way younger siblings often do, and when he proposed that I spend the summer in Nashville, I was hopeful and thought that maybe this time would be different.

And, at first, it was different. We went to parties, he let me drink beer, we worked, and played music together. He treated me like an equal for the first time ever, but in the end, he sold me out the way he always did.

We got into some trouble with the police one night on the way home from a party, and I was charged with underage drinking. I had to go to court and pay some fines. I still don't know why to this day, but he decided to tell my parents everything at the end of the summer and sent me home.

When I was about twenty, he apologized for everything he had put me through over the years, but by then, it didn't really matter. It was all just part of my story.

Today, we help each other out when we can. We see

each other at our kids' birthdays and holidays. There is love there, but we are not close.

I headed back to Massachusetts after that summer and prepared for my junior year in high school. It was my third new school in three years. Christian school was over, and I had no interest in going back to the public school in my town, so I decided to try the public school in the next town over. At this point, I had gotten my driver's license, so I was able to drive myself to school and get my old band back together.

On the first day of school, I walked into the bathroom to find a group of kids smoking. I had never been to a school where you could get away with that, and I thought, "I think I'm going to like it here."

And I did. I made some good friends, and I wasn't feeling depressed or suicidal anymore. I was still lost, angry, hurt, and confused about life, but I had a new confidence that I hadn't possessed in a while, which felt good.

There were three questions, however, that would not leave me alone and were like a thorn in my mind. You know, those three questions most of us start asking at some point in our lives. Where did I come from? What is the purpose of this life? What happens when I die?

It would be a long time before I realized that the nature of those questions was wrong. The answer is in the words.

What are words? Words are symbols that we use to represent things and ideas, but the word is not the thing or idea itself. We have become so habitual with language that maybe that was a profound statement that you just read. I know I thought it to be when I first heard it. We often confuse the word for the thing or the experience.

While we may agree on what some words mean, there are other words that I like to refer to as "loaded" words. Loaded words mean different things to different people and can lead to dangerous misunderstandings.

God, for example, is what I would call a loaded word, because the word God has so many different meanings that using it can cause conflict and division. Words are powerful. Words are thoughts manifested. Remember, "in the beginning was the word." Words can uplift and enlighten, or they can harm and cut.

As the embodiment or microcosm of the Universe, we are both darkness and light. We have the power to create things that benefit our world or harm our world. Think of nuclear power. Nuclear power can be used to create bombs that destroy. It can also be used to make electricity to make life better for millions.

So there I was in eleventh grade at a new school, feeling better but still somewhat preoccupied with some big questions. I was working full time at this point and going to school. I had worked some sort of job ever since I was very young. At first, I would mow the lawn or wash my parents' cars for extra money.

Eventually, I started delivering newspapers on my bike after school. At the end of the week, I would collect from my customers, and on Saturday, I would ride my bike down into town to the newspaper's office. I would pay what was owed, and whatever was left over would be mine to keep. I would usually go to the store and spend most of it on candy, saving just enough for a movie ticket. Then I would eat the candy while I watched the movie. I didn't know it at the time, but I was getting high on sugar.

When I was thirteen, I was able to get a work permit with my parents' permission, and I took a job washing dishes at a restaurant. It was a busy restaurant, and the dishes would pile up no matter how fast I washed them. By the end of the night, there would be a mountain of unwashed dishes that I would have to work my way through before I could go home. I washed soup pots that were so big that I would scrub them from the inside. The head cook would yell, "Where did Jordan go?" And I would wave from inside the pot, "I'm in here, boss!"

I would scrub the kitchen floor by hand, and I had to clean the bathrooms. Because of the repetitive nature of the work, I would dream at night about mountains of dishes that I couldn't wash fast enough.

Eventually, a position opened up on the line, and they started teaching me how to cook. I was only fourteen, and I loved the responsibility and working with the adults. Because I busted my ass, they treated me like an equal, not like a kid. I moved from that restaurant to another, then to another, learning more at each place and getting pay increases every time. I didn't play sports or have extracurricular activities. I worked. By the time I reached senior year in high school, I was a sous chef at a four-star restaurant.

Teaching yoga has never felt like work to me, although

I do work at it, and I do make money from teaching. But the word "work" to me means something that a person does solely to make money. When a person will do something regardless of whether they make money, then that is what I call a passion. Yoga for me is a passion. It's fortunate if one can support their family with their passion.

In yoga, we speak of *dharma*. *Dharma* is one's duty. All of us have a reason for our existence; something we were brought into this life to do, something the Universe wants to do as me. We are meant to discover our *dharma* and learn in the process of executing it.

By the time I was a junior in high school, I hadn't discovered my *dharma* yet, but I had a full-time job with benefits, my own car, money for weed and dates with girls, and I was still getting straight A's in school. But I could not stop questioning authority. I was always looking for ways to rebel and cause trouble.

One of my fellow delinquents wore a shirt to school one day with a pentagram on it and was sent to the principal's office. The principal told him to turn it inside out and return to class. When I found out about it, I went down to the principal's office and told him he couldn't do that. I said, "This is a public school! We don't have uniforms! If he has to turn his shirt inside out, then anyone who is wearing a cross around their neck, or any other symbol, should have to remove it as well."

He said, "It is a disruption to class because some of the students find it offensive." I then told him that I found the cross offensive, and he told me to go back to class.

I went back to class and formulated a plan. He wasn't going to brush me off that easily. That afternoon, I made arm bands with pentagrams on them and handed them out to all of my friends, and the next day, we all wore them to school in protest. They gave us all two-day in school suspensions, and for two days, I sat in a room at school by myself.

I thought, "I know what would make this more interesting!" I dropped some acid and took out my colored pencils. It was supposed to be punishment, but those were the two most entertaining days I ever had at school.

I was cocky, arrogant, and angry, not good qualities in anyone, but the girls didn't seem to mind. The girl from the Christian school was my first serious girlfriend. We were sweet on each other for a while, but in the end, she broke it off with me on my birthday while I was away in Nashville with my brother. There were other girls here and there, but nothing serious until… let's call her Lenore.

Chapter Five

I didn't lay eyes on her until the end of Junior year, but the first time she strutted past me in that short skirt with those thighs and those eyes, BAM! I was smitten. I practically fell over trying to get up and chase her down the hall. I asked her her name and chatted her up. She smiled. She had a keen wit and a sharp tongue.

I found out later that she had known exactly what she was doing that day when she walked by me. By her own admission she had been trying to catch my eye, and it had worked; hook, line, and sinker. She had me, and we were pretty much inseparable after that.

Lenore and her three sisters lived with their mom. Their dad had been MIA most of their lives, and their mom had become jaded about his absence. She had made every effort to ruin Lenore's impression of him and men in general. I am not saying I blame her for that. If I had to raise three daughters all by myself, I might be a little jaded too.

I consider myself a feminist in the sense that I believe that women deserve equal rights, representation, and pay, but Lenore was the kind of feminist that at some deep level hated men and was incapable of ever fully trusting one. For the seven years we were together, this fact worked against us. I continually worked to gain her trust, but I don't think I ever did.

She was very intelligent; so smart, in fact, that she skipped senior year and graduated high school the same year I did. She knew how to inflame my reckless nature, and we had some interesting adventures. Lenore's relationship with her mother was strained by our relationship and the trouble we would get into, and my relationship with my family had been terrible for years.

Because I had been working as a sous chef, my parents and college counselors encouraged me to apply to a culinary program for college. I did and was accepted at Johnson and Wales University. On the 4th of July that summer, however, I changed my mind.

I was working that night, as I did on most holidays and weekends. I remember sitting out behind the restaurant smoking a cigarette and wishing I was headed to watch the fireworks like everyone else. I asked myself, "Is this what you want to do with your life? Working and serving so that everyone else can have a good time?" The answer was, "No."

At this point, Lenore had made contact with her father, who was living with his wife in Guilford, Surrey, outside of London. He invited us to come and use his house as a base to do some traveling around England and other parts of Europe. When I told my parents that I was going to England instead of college, and that I didn't know when I would be back, they were surprisingly supportive of the idea.

I had been working and saving money, as had Lenore, and between the two of us, we had about five thousand dollars. We decided to buy two one-way tickets to London, and converted the rest of our money to traveler's checks.

Lenore had one of her friends drive us to the airport the day we were leaving, and looking back, I believe he was the first of many people she would cheat on me with, but at that point, I had no idea.

We got to the gate just in time that night and were off on the adventure of a lifetime. We arrived in London the following morning. Lenore's father and stepmother picked us up and took us back to their flat; a cute little two-bedroom with a lovely garden in the back.

Lenore's father, Walter, and his wife, Caroline, were cool and very accepting. They wanted us to like them. Walter and I connected over the fact that we were both trying to earn Lenore's trust, and he turned out to be an interesting fellow.

He was a nudist who drank beer and smoked hash, and in the morning when I woke up, I would find him sitting at the kitchen table reading, buck naked. He would look up and smile as if nothing was amiss and offer me coffee. We went to some nudist events and beaches with them, which I found to be funny and quirky. Naked humans didn't make me uncomfortable, and I had no issues with being naked myself. I liked Walter and Caroline very much and enjoyed our time together.

After some time in London, Lenore and I decided to buy Eurobus passes, and with these passes, we could travel wherever we wanted. A bus traveled in a loop passing through each city every couple of days. We could explore each city, stay in each place for as long as we liked, and then hop on the bus when we were ready to move on. We had six months to complete the route and opted for the Northern European one.

We began by taking a ferry across the English channel and, once on the other side, headed to Paris! We visited the Louvre, Jim Morrisons's grave, and watched the sunset from the Eiffel Tower. Paris was expensive, however, and I was anxious to get to Amsterdam, so after two days, we moved onto Brussels.

When you are young and traveling like this, you constantly meet people; people on the bus, people at the hostels.

During our one and only night in Brussels, there were about seven or eight of us representing different countries sitting around the common room at the hostel drinking beer and talking. At some point, the conversation shifted, lord knows how, to the American Revolutionary War. The Brits in the group knew it as the Colonial Rebellion; as did the people from Australia and South Africa, both former British colonies. This is when I learned that history is mostly subjective.

History is often told to put the teller in a positive light. Up until this conversation, I believed history to be objective. I mean the facts were the facts, right? But often, that is not the case. I took this new perspective to Amsterdam, a place of legend that I had heard about my entire drug-using life and was dying to get to.

Marijuana was illegal in the United States at the time, but not in Amsterdam. We planned to spend two weeks there and arrived right in the middle of spring break for European colleges. The city was a madhouse. People were partying everywhere, some passed out in the streets with their packs on. I watched one guy mistake the turn on his bicycle and drive straight off a bridge into the filthy canal.

All the hostels were full, and we wandered around the city trying to find a place to spend the night. This innocent girl walked up and asked where the Christian Youth Hostel was. I laughed and said, "Be careful asking that question! You don't know who you are talking to."

I thought it was going to be so much fun. I had all these grand ideas of what it would be like, but I spent most of our time there high, lost, and paranoid. I didn't know the laws or the culture. I didn't know what was legal or illegal, safe or unsafe, socially acceptable or socially awkward. I felt like a disrespectful intruder, and I suppose I was.

In the end, after four days, I grabbed Lenore by the shoulders, looked her in the eyes and said, "We have to get out of here. I need to get on the bus in the morning. I can't handle this place." I couldn't. I was too immature and out of control. I felt so relieved once we were on the bus, driving out of the city. I thought, "I did it! I survived Amsterdam!"

I would go back many years later for Angela's thirtieth birthday and have a very different experience. It's actually a beautiful city. I would love to retire there someday and live on a nice little houseboat with a cat.

You see how that works? Thought, that is. Do you know what you are doing when you are thinking? What is a thought? What is Truth? What is reality? Are they the same? What is the relationship between them? Are you having trouble answering these questions?

I wouldn't be surprised if you were. They don't teach us this stuff in school, although they should. We should all

45

be able to answer these questions as easily as we can answer 2+2. I mean, you think all the time, and yet you don't know what you are actually doing when you are doing it. Doesn't that seem odd to you?

We use the words mind, brain, and consciousness like they are interchangeable, like they all mean the same thing. But do they? Why have three words then? Just for variety? Surely not. So why, then? Could it be that each one expresses some subtle difference? Allow me to explain.

Brain is the organ of the mind. Mind is the combination of sense experience, memory, and time. Consciousness operates the mind when things are working properly. A thought is when awareness accesses the contents of the mind; calculating, analyzing, and predicting. Where are *you* in this process? What do *you* refer to as yourself? Is that your brain, your mind, your thoughts, or a combination of them? Are you your body?

Reality is subjective. Like history, it depends upon an individual's perspective. Truth, on the other hand, is objective. The Truth is. When a person is having an experience, any experience, there is information coming into the brain through our senses.

Now, if a person were to have that same experience without thought, as I just defined it, the person would be perceiving. Pure perception is the absence of thought. It is just the experience of the senses. The more extreme the experience, the more likely it is that the person will commit it to memory. The more routine or ordinary the experience, the more likely we will not commit it to memory.

What is contained in memory? The contents of memory includes knowledge, beliefs, experience, and preference. Knowledge is everything we have been taught through education, culture, and tradition; every book we have ever read, every TV program we have ever seen. Beliefs are determined by whether or not we agree with this knowledge that we have been taught. Experience is everything our body has experienced through the senses. The last one, preference, is the sticky one.

Preference can cause many complications, and most of us don't even realize what is happening, because we don't understand thought. Every time we commit something to memory, we slap a label on the memory. If we enjoyed it, we label it "pleasure." If don't like it, we label it "pain." These labels have a tremendous amount of significance in our lives. They influence every decision we make and every action we take.

Most children are raised in a reward and punishment model. If we do the "right thing," what our families and society want us to do, then we are rewarded. If we go against that, we are punished. So we grow up to be adults who are forever chasing pleasure and trying to avoid pain.

Furthermore, when we are children, we don't have a huge storehouse of memory. Because of that, we mostly perceive the present moment without thought. As we grow and gain more and more experiences, we spend more time thinking and less time perceiving. So what are we doing when we are thinking? Well, we are essentially time traveling.

Physical time is distance. It takes time to travel from here to there. It is the distance our Earth travels around the sun, broken into smaller and smaller increments. Psychological time is different. Psychological time is yesterday, today, and tomorrow. Yesterday, today, and tomorrow is all the brain knows.

Anything that we have already experienced in the past is yesterday. If I were to ask you to recall some experience from when you were ten years old, intellectually, you would understand that it happened ten, twenty, thirty, forty years ago, but experiencing the memory would feel like yesterday. Isn't that what we always say? "I remember it like it was yesterday." That is because in our psychological perception of time, it was yesterday. As we perceive it, all of the past was yesterday.

The present is today. As Oogway from *Kung-Fu Panda* said, "Today is a gift, that is why it's called the present." The present moment is today. The *now* is what we understand as today. I love the saying, "Why put off to tomorrow what you can do today?" Even though I can be a huge procrastinator, there is so much truth in that statement. Here is the deal. Even the next moment is tomorrow, and tomorrow might not come to you.

There is no guarantee of the future. We all go about our lives as if the next moment is a given, until it isn't, and then we are shocked by the truth of our own mortality. Maybe you do have many more tomorrows, or maybe tomorrow will never come for you. If we hold onto this Truth, we are likely to live fully.

We can remember yesterday, and we can understand continuity and tomorrow, but we can't live in either one. We cannot act or create in any way to affect the past. We also have no control over the future. We struggle with this. We think we can plan and predict the future with thought, and sometimes we do have some success in bringing our plans to fruition, but in truth, we have no control over the future. Convincing ourselves that we have control over the future causes so much suffering.

The present, on the other hand, is where we have all the divine power of consciousness and creativity. That is why it is a gift. Now is when we can do, act, and create. Now is when we can affect change. Change is constant. It is always happening. Now is where we have the power to affect the change. So, then, what are we doing when we are thinking?

When we are thinking, we are going into the past and accessing memory, and then comparing these memories to the present moment's sensory experiences, and then making decisions about the future based on these comparisons. In other words, we spend today remembering yesterday and planning tomorrow. In this way, we are always viewing the present through the lens of our preferences.

When we have a pure experience of the present, we are not thinking about it, because there is nothing in memory to compare it to. We mostly perceive the present moment when we are young. As we age, we accumulate more and more memories, and gradually perceive less, and think more. It happens so slowly that we don't consciously register this shift taking place.

If we are thinking about the present moment, then we are experiencing it through the filter of our memories and not experiencing it as it is. We experience a distortion, and this distortion is our individual reality. This reality may or may not have anything to do with what is True. It's all because of our preferences.

I don't want you to just read these words as knowledge. Test it for yourself and see. The seeing is the doing. If the present situation or set of circumstances is similar to any memory, then the brain will make this information available to intelligence.

If the memory is labeled "pleasure," then we try to recreate the experience to re-experience that pleasure, and this formulates desire. The desire for pleasure in the future is called hope.

If the memory is labeled "pain," then we begin to predict actions we can take to avoid repeating the pain, which also formulates desire. The desire to avoid pain is called fear. Hope and fear stem from the same root: desire. The cause of desire is memory and preference.

When I am recalling my memories of Amsterdam, I have one memory labeled "pain" and the other labeled "pleasure". When I said I would like to retire there someday and have a nice houseboat and a cat, I was taking the pleasurable memory and projecting it into the future as hope. If I had projected the "painful" memory of Amsterdam into the future as fear, I would have said something like, "I'm never going back to that place. It's scary and not for me."

In Daniel Kahneman's book, *Thinking, Fast and Slow*, he explains all this in terms of "System 1 and System 2," although Dr. Seuss's "Thing 1 and Thing 2" might be more appropriate. In the yoga model, they are called *manomaya kosha* (mind illusion sheath) and *vijñānamaya kosha* (intellect illusion sheath).

I refer to them as memory and intellect. Memory is quick to react to stimulation. Almost immediately after the stimulus is there, the brain will quickly spit out any associated memory content. Intellect is slower to respond, and if not exercised regularly, will become lazy and default to memory.

For example, I ask you the question, "Roses are…?" If you immediately responded "red", then that is memory. The problem with memory as you can see is that it is often biased and incomplete. Roses can be red, but they can also be pink, white, or yellow. So why did you respond, "red"? You responded that way because your memory just spit out the answer instantly, and intellect didn't intervene.

Now, if I ask you the question, "Violets are…?" and you immediately answer, "blue," then that is memory once again. If instead, you paused and used your intellect to answer the question, you might find that you come up with a different answer, such as violet or purple. If the question does not stand out to you as different or unique, most of the time, memory will answer automatically, and intellect will stay quiet.

If I asked you, "Can you step into the same river twice?" and you quickly answer "Yes, of course," that is memory answering. If you pause, think about your answer, realize that the river is always moving and so it is never the "same," and respond, "No," then you are using your intellect. Understand? Memory is automatic. Intellect is deliberative. Intellect must be exercised regularly, questioning everything that comes out of memory for validity.

If a person operates only from memory, then they are just reacting, and repeating the same actions over and over again. This is called *saṃskāra* (mental impressions) in

51

sanskrit. If a person is operating from intellect, then they are responding to each situation separately and consciously. This is what the Buddhists refer to as mindfulness. See what I meant earlier when I said that mindfulness is time between stimulus and response? Space in the mind for intellect to observe memory and choose.

In terms of memory and intellect, I'm not sure where I was at when we left Amsterdam, but when we arrived at the German border, I was swiftly forced into the present moment. With no previous memories of military men carrying machine guns, intellect was all I had. These men boarded our bus and began to check everyone's passports.

A Scottish bloke, sitting in front of us with a bunch of hash and valium, panicked at the sight of the German soldiers. Fearing prison, he ingested all the drugs. The Germans ended up passing over him, as they were only concerned with U.S. passports. He passed out, and we were so concerned that he was going to die of an overdose, but he slept it off and was fine by the time we got to Berlin.

I got my lip pierced in Berlin, and then we moved onto Prague, which turned out to be the unexpected jewel of the trip. I had no previous knowledge of the Czech Republic, and so no expectations. This was 1997 and pre-European Union, and each country had their own currency. The Czech crown was trading at ten crown to one USD, and one crown spent like one USD. At these prices, we could afford an apartment with a jacuzzi, and a liter of beer was about ten cents!

The city had beautiful medieval architecture, the people were friendly, and we ended up spending a couple of weeks there. I drank Absinthe without the sugar cube because I didn't know any better, and it burned like gasoline from my lips to my stomach. I immediately cramped, but after that, a warm feeling followed, and then it was a blur of reckless drunkenness. I remember fighting with a mailbox. Why? I have no idea. "That mailbox is looking at me funny. Hey! You got a problem mailbox?!"

After Prague, we went to Vienna, and after that, Kirchdorf. Snowboarding in the Alps in the spring is one of the most stunning experiences this planet has to offer. It would be snowing at the top, and we would ride down into green valleys that were seventy degrees.

Then, we passed back into Germany, stopping in Munich. I got drunk in a beer hall, ate amazing pretzels, and the bus driver had to more or less carry me back to the hostel. Nice fella, that bus driver. I wish I could remember his name. Anyway, cheers mate! Thanks for getting us home that night.

In Switzerland, I scored some hash from some crazy skater kids. It didn't matter what country or city we went to, I never had problems finding cannabis. In most cases, people would walk right up to me and ask what I needed. Maybe it was the piercings and the tattoos? Maybe it was the black leather jacket with the metal spikes? Maybe it was the steel-toed Doc Martens? Maybe it was a combination of all those things, but something about my appearance just screamed, "Drugs! Drugs over here please!"

We left Geneva and headed back to Paris, and from there on to London. We spent a couple of weeks hiking around England, and then we headed to the island of Skiathos in Greece.

The only thing to do there was hang out on the beach

at the resort, shoot pool, and drink. Every morning, I would wake up with a crippling hangover. I would lay on the beach and swear that I wasn't going to do it again, but then I would feel better after dinner and start drinking. I still can't stand the smell of tequila twenty years later.

Finally, the time came for us to head back to the states. We were running out of funds, so we bought two tickets on India Air, the cheapest tickets we could find. That flight from London to New York was the first and only flight I would ever take that still allowed smoking on the plane. We arrived in New York, our international adventures over, and from there, hopped a bus to Boston. It was time to head back to normal life.

Chapter Six

Returning home after six months of total freedom was rather unpleasant, and I was determined to get my own apartment as soon as possible. Lenore was going to college, and I needed a roommate. I wound up taking a two-bedroom apartment in Natick, MA with a friend from high school and his girlfriend. Lenore had to live on campus freshman year, but she would take the train out and stay with me on the weekends.

I had used up all my money traveling, so I started working two full-time jobs. I would work five a.m. to two p.m. at Starbucks, grab a nap in my car for an hour, and then work three p.m. to eleven p.m. in the kitchen at the Olive Garden. I had two days off from each job, but for whatever reason, I never had the same days off for both. I would sometimes have a morning or a night off, but never a whole day. I worked seven days a week, and it was exhausting,

One night at the Olive Garden, the manager invited me out behind the dumpster to smoke a joint. It was some really good stuff, and so I asked if he could get me some. The next day, he handed me an ounce, and I was like, "Whoa, no, that's way too much. I can't afford that."

He said, "You have friends, don't you?"

"Yeah?" I replied, confused by the question.

"Take it, sell it, smoke some, and pay me later," he said. And just like that, I became a drug dealer.

I sold the first ounce in a day, so I paid him and got two more, and then four more, and so on. Every time I bought more, the price went down, and I made more profit. Eventually, I started getting a couple pounds at a time and paying upfront, which again lowered my costs.

Between the two jobs and the dealing, I was really making a lot of money, but I was being incredibly reckless and stupid about it. I had people showing up at the house at all hours; people I didn't even know. It's a miracle that I didn't get robbed or arrested.

After about a year, I was at my breaking point, and one night at the Olive Garden, I just snapped. I couldn't do it anymore. I took off my apron and left that life and never went back to cooking again. My lease was up, and I had some friends who wanted to get a place in Boston, so I moved to the city.

My first apartment in Boston was a magical place. We rented the top floor of a typical Boston three-family home in the neighborhood of Allston. Allston was, is, and probably always will be a young, hip part of the city with lots of college students and immigrants; a lovely and diverse neighborhood. There were four of us: Tom, Kelly, Lenore, and me.

The front room of the place was a big, bright affair with three windows where we set up all of our computers, so it looked something like an internet cafe. There were two couches arranged on the opposite side with a large space in between for dancing and socializing.

We mounted a six-foot blacklight to the ceiling and hung glow-in-the-dark stars from strings. We would put all four computer monitors on the "Flying Through Space" screensaver, and we called the room "Space Camp." There was even a little roof that could be reached by crawling out one of the windows, and I used to smoke out there and watch the sunrise.

Tom and Kelly were party kids. They were my introduction to rave culture and the drug methylenedioxy-methamphetamine (MDMA or Molly). We just called it ecstasy, or simply X. They took Lenore and me to our first rave at a place called The Metropolis in the middle of nowhere Maine.

I remember standing in a mob of people waiting to get inside. When we got to the front, the bouncer at the door commented that they were already at twice the capacity, but, "not to worry, we would all get in." And we did.

Any rational person would have wondered about the safety of that, but that didn't occur to me. The entire place was black-lit, and everything glowed. DJ Dan was spinning, and the place was packed to the gills and bumping. It was so hot in there, and the cinder block walls were so cold because it was winter, in Maine, that it actually started raining *inside!*

We wound up "candy flipping" that night. That's when you take LSD (lysergic acid diethylamide) and ecstasy together, and it was hands down my favorite drug experience. I experienced all the awesome hallucinations without the edgy side effects. Everything was colorful and happy. It was the closest thing to rainbows, unicorns, and fairies I have ever experienced.

P.L.U.R. sums up rave culture. It stands for peace, love, unity, and respect, and to me, it feels like utopia. For someone who was constantly angry and railing against the world, this culture was a breath of fresh air, and it changed me. I saw how good things could be in this existence, when we all love and respect each other.

At one point during the night, I was chatting and smoking with someone when Tom came running up to me with a drawing pad of paper. He held up a blank page in front of me and said, "Look!" I thought he had totally lost it.

"Look at what?" I said. "It's a blank piece of paper."

He insisted that I look at it, so I looked again, and this time, things began to appear on the blank piece of paper; colors, then shapes and forms.

I sat there dumbfounded, watching all manner of things manifesting there for what seemed like hours, but was really more like minutes, until I suddenly remembered that I was only looking at a blank piece of paper. Everything I was "seeing" was just in my head. I laughed myself silly, and after that night at The Metropolis, I was sold. This was a community I wanted to be a part of. These are my people.

I wish I could say that the experience ended my anger, but it didn't. It did, however, alleviate it for a few hours, and I experienced a level of connectedness that I had not previously known was possible. Years later, I heard a quote from Ram Das who said, "I wasn't addicted to the drugs. I was obsessed with the feeling of connection and wholeness they gave me." I would agree with that. It was never about the drugs for me. It was about what the drugs allowed me to experience.

It was around this time that Matthew walked into my life. There are some people in your life who, when you meet them for the first time, you just know your life will never be the same. And Matthew was one of those people.

If you have never worked for Starbucks, then you probably don't know that they only need to sell one cup of coffee out of every urn to make money, and we were instructed to throw out each urn after an hour to make sure the coffee was always fresh. Because of this, there was an unspoken rule that it was okay to give your friends free coffee.

When Matthew came rolling into my Starbucks one morning looking like a real hustler with two beautiful ladies, one on each arm, I thought to myself, I don't know who this guy is, but he's doing something right! I need to get to know him!

They ordered their coffees, and when it was time to pay, I told them they were all set. They were surprised, and grateful. I smiled and sent them on their way. Every time they came in, while I was working, they didn't pay, and, over time, we became friends.

Matthew walked his dogs at the park behind my apartment, and I would chat with him there sometimes whenever we crossed paths. Through our conversations, I learned that Matthew and his friends worked at a trendy clothing store on Newbury Street, where everyone went to buy their fancy clothes for the nightclubs.

At this point, I had become obsessed with electronic music, nightclubs, and rave culture, and I really wanted to work at one of the clubs in Boston. When I learned that the clothing store was hiring, I thought that maybe I would meet someone working there who could get me a job in a club.

I told my roommate, Tom, that I was going to apply for a job there, and he decided to apply too. Tom was kind of a nerdy, intellectual guy, and I believed that I was way cooler than him. I thought for sure they would pick me, but unfortunately, Matthew did not do the hiring, and Tom got the job. I was pretty disappointed.

Time went by, and I continued working at Starbucks and selling weed until one day when I had just finished the opening shift at Starbucks and had arrived home. I sat down and flipped on the TV when the phone rang. Matthew was on the other end, and he was looking for Tom. I guess Tom had confused his schedule for the week, and he was supposed to be at work.

I knew that Tom thought he had the day off and had gone out into the woods to eat magic mushrooms with some friends. I saw an opportunity, and I decided to go for it. I said to Matthew, "I know there is no way Tom can come to work today, but I just finished my shift at Starbucks, and I can be there in thirty minutes if you need someone." And that was it. I had my in. I nervously changed my clothes, jumped on the train, and got myself down there.

They told me to organize the shoe room, and I did exactly what they told me to do, as fast as I could. The scary manager lady came in to check on my work looking annoyed with obviously low expectations. When she saw what I had done in such a short amount of time, she grudgingly mustered a "Good job." When she walked out, I breathed a huge sigh of relief. I had passed the first test.

I found out that day that they were planning on opening a new store that would sell rave fashion. They promised me a position at the new store when it opened. Matthew and his roommate, Sarah, were going to be manager and assistant manager. I was thrilled.

That store was my Empire Records, if you have ever seen the film. It brought together a ragtag motley crew of characters, and we all became fast friends. We worked hard and partied harder. Paul Oakenfold's *Global Underground: New York* became our soundtrack.

Matthew was the son of a wealthy businessman. He had a car and owned a condo. He and his roommate, Sarah, were a few years older than the rest of us. I became part of his crew and was now rolling into Starbucks with them on our way to work, strung out from the previous night's festivities. I looked up to Matthew like a big brother. He taught me so many things, and, under his tutelage, I learned how to sell, how to party hard and function socially, and how to handle my business before I play.

We would open the store, crank the music, and sell like crazy. Then we would close the store and go back to Matthew's place and party. I'd eventually go home, sleep it off, wake up, and do it all over again.

Ecstasy was primarily our drug of choice during this period, which would explain why we all became so close. I had found a reliable source where I could buy in bulk and reduce the cost. I had a constant parade of potential customers, and management was willing to look the other way.

I would sell each pill for about three times what I paid for it, so I was making a ton of money, and able to keep a bunch of pills for myself and the group. Marijuana was always smoked, and occasionally, when available, we would take ketamine, LSD, or magic mushrooms.

For the most part, I avoided drugs like cocaine and heroin because of their addictive nature. I knew I would enjoy them, and probably end up dead, so I stayed away. That was until I met Tina. Tina was not a person. Tina is what we called crystalized methamphetamine.

Back in 1999, crystal meth was not something that was in the news. Nobody really knew what it was. I certainly had no idea that it was potentially so addictive. The first time I tried it, I felt more sober than I had ever been in my entire life. It made my brain work at a level of efficiency that I had never before experienced, like the pill in the movie, Limitless. I could see the strings that controlled the system. I felt like I could do anything. And at first, that is how I functioned. I would stay up for days working, talking, and playing video games.

We were never people who would steal or hurt other people to get more drugs. We took pride in being functional drug users. I worked to buy my drugs, and when the money or the drugs ran out, which they inevitably always did, I was usually ready to come down. I would go home and sleep it off, sweat out the sheets, detox, shower, eat, and then get back to work, and do it all over again.

We viewed most other people like sheep. We felt superior. It was always about what we could get away with without anyone else knowing. We would get totally fucked up, and then go out in public and keep it together enough so that none of the squares knew. That was the game. Getting out of control was frowned upon. We were a tight-knit group of attractive, intelligent people, and everywhere we went, people knew us, and we attracted attention. I felt like the world was my playground and anything was possible.

Chapter Seven

My obsession with electronic music led me to the New England Institute of Art, where I began a program in sound engineering. I'd eventually complete an associate's degree and acquire the skills I needed to become a music producer and sound engineer. This is also where I met Jack.

Jack was to me what I was to Matthew. He was my little bro. He was a little bit younger, had the best ears for sound engineering in the school, and he looked up to me and the way I operated in the world. I took him under my wing and brought him into our crew. Meanwhile, back at Space Camp, things were rapidly deteriorating.

What had started out as utopia was decaying into a place I didn't want to be. Lenore and I were always fighting. She didn't like Matthew because she lost her control over me when I was with him. She had taken an apprenticeship with a master mason and had started shagging one of the guys she worked with. She frequently would not come home, claiming it was because of the drive. I didn't buy it. I knew she was cheating, even though she wouldn't admit it.

Tom and Kelly were on the outs, too. I was becoming increasingly attracted to Kelly, but she wasn't interested. Tom didn't have the mental fortitude to keep up with the pace of the drug use and had a couple of psychotic breaks.

He never hurt anyone, but he definitely went a little crazy. After babysitting him through it a couple of times, I was done with him. I saw him as weak. He couldn't keep up. I wanted to be with people who could keep their shit together, not people I had to babysit. Tom and Kelly broke up, Tom went back to live with his parents, and Kelly found a studio apartment for herself.

Lenore and I could not afford Space Camp by ourselves, but we also couldn't afford to live alone. We broke up too, but decided to get a two-bedroom apartment in the same building as Kelly and live together as friends with separate rooms.

This was the worst apartment I had ever lived in. It was dirty when we moved in. The ceilings were only six feet high, and the ceiling tiles were all stained. There was dust and mold, and all the walls were crooked and the floors were sloped. It should have been condemned.

What goes up, must come down. I had been living the high life for two years. I was now on the downslope of things, and I knew it. When the wheel of *saṃsāra* turns, we all feel it.

Saṃsāra is the wheel of life; the cycle of death and rebirth to which all life in the material world is bound. As the wheel turns, things change, just like the changing of the seasons on the Earth. As the Earth turns, we ride this wheel, which gives life its ups and downs. Picture a wagon wheel. There's the outer circle of the wheel, and the inner circle at the hub where the axle goes. The outer circle is connected to the inner circle by spokes.

Most of us are riding on the outer circle. When we are on the top of the wheel, we are riding high and feeling good.

We feel like we are on top of the world. When the wheel turns, we feel the shift. We can tell things are going down, and we don't like where we are headed. We start feeling apprehensive. We begin projecting our desire to avoid pain into the future, creating fear and anxiety, which clouds our judgment and affects our actions and behaviors.

Then, the wheel turns again, and we find ourselves at the bottom of the wheel, being crushed between the weight of the world and the ground of being. We begin to project into the future a desire for our pain to be alleviated, and we create hope. Once again, this hope is a distortion. It is a reality that may or may not be True.

The wheel continues to turn relentlessly, never stopping, never hesitating, until we find ourselves on the uptrend. We can feel the weight and pressure ease on us. We become optimistic and begin to look ahead to better times. Projecting a desire for pleasure in the future, we hope the wheel will continue to turn, and when it does, we find ourselves back on top again, riding high.

Most of us ride this wheel over and over and over. It's a fun ride, until it isn't. Most of us just accept this. It is only when a person begins to ask, "Is this the way life has to be?" that a person begins to wake up. This is the beginning of yoga. I often ask my students, "What is the goal of yoga? What is the intended purpose of these practices? What are we trying to accomplish by doing this?"

Because most people still think of yoga as exercise or fitness, the most common responses I hear to those questions are of a physical nature. They'll say, "I want to get stronger," or "I want to get healthier."

It's funny because these are also the most common

responses to why people *don't* do yoga. People always say things like, "I can't do yoga because I'm not flexible enough," which always makes me laugh. My typical response to that is, "So, what you're saying is that you are too dirty to take a bath?"

It is true. Yoga *asānas* will make you stronger and more flexible, but that was not why they were created. Becoming flexible and strong are simply beneficial side effects of yoga. Some of my more experienced students might give responses to those questions from the mental or energetic levels of their experiences. They will say things like, "I want to be healthy" or "I want to balance my emotions" or "I want to calm my mind."

All of these things will happen through the practices of yoga, but they are not the goal. These are simply things that happen along the path to yoga.

In the East, no matter what school or sect of yoga tradition one follows, the goal is always the same. The goal is liberation. Liberation from suffering. Liberation from the suffering that is caused from riding the wheel of *saṃsāra*. This is the purpose of yoga regardless of the practitioner's intention. If practiced diligently, for an extended period of time, liberation from suffering is what will result.

Know yoga, know peace. No yoga, no peace. This discrepancy between East and West is because of how yoga has been packaged and sold to us in the West. When you say yoga in the West, most people think of the *asānas*. To them, that is yoga. They don't realize that there are seven other practices that comprise the whole of classical yoga.

In the East, people associate the word yoga with seated meditation, spirituality, and religion, but by stripping the practice down to only the physical, most dense layer of human existence, it makes yoga more accessible to Westerners.

Regardless of one's motivations for doing yoga, if done for long enough, the intended purpose will begin to make itself evident. That is to say, a person may come to yoga for six pack abs and a tight butt, but if they keep doing it, they will wind up finding liberation. This has certainly been my experience. I had no idea what I was getting into when I went to my first yoga class.

One night, when Matthew and I were closing up the store and writing down the day's sales totals in the ledger like we did every night at closing, Matthew launched the idea of opening our own store. I mean, after all, we were doing all of the work, right? Why shouldn't *we* be making the profits? Matthew decided he would ask his father for a loan to start the store.

In order to do that, he knew he would have to show his father that he was serious, so we all got to work on creating a business plan. Each of us in the clan had specific duties based upon our individual strengths; strengths that we hoped would turn into lucrative jobs in the future. We found brands that no other stores were selling, that we believed were going to take off. We calculated build-out costs. We created pie charts and graphs, analyzing potential market share and revenue, and Matthew already had a name that he had been thinking about for some time.

We worked as hard as we partied, and that's saying something. I have never attended business school, but in my humble opinion, this crazy band of misfits had put together a solid business plan, and I believed that with some capital and hard work, we could be successful. That capital never came through, though, so I guess I will never know.

When the time came for Matthew to go home and speak with his father, we put him on a plane, wished him luck, and waited. Optimism was high. I was hopeful, but realistic. I knew what my motivations were. I loved these people. I was inspired.

We were like a family of sorts, and I was fanatical in my loyalty to Matthew. I would have done just about anything for him. He was the best friend and brother I'd ever known. He wanted his own store, and I would do everything in my power to help him get it. I hoped that it would all work out and that we would all get rich, but the camaraderie was the most important thing to me.

I also felt like I had nothing to lose. Nothing ventured, nothing gained, right? I did not anticipate that I would lose big. I did not anticipate that I would lose my best friend.

I don't know what happened when Matthew went back home. That is his memory, not mine. My memory is of me sitting in the back seat of his car, on the trip back from the airport, looking at his eyes in the rear-view mirror. Something in his eyes had changed. They were always so piercingly intense, like he wasn't looking at me, but was looking right into my soul. Now, he didn't even want to look at me. His language was very short and tight. He felt distant and cold.

It turned out that Matthew's father was in some

financial trouble with his own company and wanted Matthew to come home and help with the business. Because of this, Matthew had never even shown him our business plan. The dream was over. But I was okay with it. I had known it was a long shot all along. I tried to comfort my friend and let him know that it was okay, but he was having none of it. I think that in his mind, he had let us all down, and he felt defeated, but I don't know, because he wouldn't talk to me about it.

After that, he quit working at the store and more or less pushed us all away. I was crushed. I felt used. Was he ever really my friend? Was it all a scam that I had fallen for? I have always considered myself to be too trusting. I don't know why, but it never even occurs to me that someone might be lying to me until I'm slapped in the face with the truth of it. Even dry humor goes right over my head. I'm just far too literal, I guess. I've never been good at innuendos or reading between the lines. I'm far too blunt. I expect people to say what they mean and mean what they say, even though I know that truly genuine people are rare.

I felt betrayed by Matthew, and, without him as our captain, our crew fell apart. After Matthew quit the store, they brought on a new manager for whom I had no respect. I was the assistant manager, and I felt they should have made me manager, so I quit as well. I landed a job doing coat check at an after-hours nightclub from midnight to five a.m. on the weekends, got my bartending license, and started working at a shoe store while still going to school. My anger was at an all-time high, but I was far too busy to examine it. I went back to operating under the motto, "I'm pissed off, and the whole world owes me!"

Lenore had been bugging me to get back together and, since no one would date me because I was still living with her, I relented. Months went by without any contact from Matthew. I continued working in the after-hours club, hoping to get a better position, maybe a more creative opportunity. A couple of guys who were working security there were starting a promotions company and needed a name, so I offered up the name of our store. I figured at least they could get some use out of it. They loved the name and eventually asked me to design a video system for the club that I would get to control every Friday during their events. I put in a video system, they printed flyers and promoted it all over Boston, and Friday nights at the club were a success.

The owners were happy, which gave me space to expand into more illicit opportunities. When I offered them a cut of the night's drug sales, they'd gladly opened their palms and looked the other way. This gave me free rein to flood the place with ecstasy, which of course made the party better and more popular. I had done it. I had my job in a club. I was making a ton of cash, but I still felt like I was being crushed by the wheel.

I was trapped in a relationship of convenience with someone I didn't want to be with. I'd lost most of my meaningful friendships, and my drug use had taken a turn. I wasn't using to feel connected anymore. I was using to medicate my rage.

The flyers were all over town, but it never even occurred to me that Matthew would see them. One of the few good things about the apartment building I was living in at the time was that we had roof access, and that year, I decided to throw myself a birthday party on the roof, complete with lights and a DJ.

To my surprise, Matthew showed up. I wanted to be mad at him, but he had brought me a present. How can you be mad at someone when they are handing you a birthday present? He was extending an olive branch, and I wasn't about to slap it away. He had bought me a Nintendo 64 game console. Playing video games together had always been a big part of our friendship.

Matthew proceeded to tell me that he had seen the flyers around town and knew I'd been the one to give them the name. Even though he felt like I had "pissed on his painting," he was not angry with me. He told me that even though I was always angry and raging against the world, he knew there was no malice in my heart. He knew that I had not given the name away in spite, but out of pain and apathy, which was true.

And that was it. We were friends again; a little older, a little wiser, and much healthier. I didn't worship him anymore. I still respected him, but our friendship was different. We didn't work together anymore, so we didn't see each other every day, but we made time to hang out often. It felt good to have him back.

Chapter Eight

That summer came to an end, and in September, Lenore, Kelly, my friend Jenny from the clothing store, and myself all moved into the first floor of a three-family house in the Mission Hill area of Boston, near Northeastern University.

This was a relatively good period for me. We were happy living together. We would all go to the club on the weekends, and I would run the video, and Kelly became one of my top sellers. She had this giant stuffed python puppet that she would wear around her neck. She kept all the pills up inside the puppet head of the snake, which made her easy to point out on the dance floor. If anyone was looking for stuff, all I had to do was say, "Go find the girl with the big snake." She would reach into the snake, pull out the X, and then the customers would feed their cash to the snake. With the security guards in my pocket, it was about as safe as dealing drugs could be.

I had accomplished all I had set out to achieve, but it didn't feel the way I had expected it to feel. I had thought that working at a nightclub would be magical, a non-stop party full of love and happiness, but it was quite the opposite. That's the problem with expectations. The Truth of a thing is often not what we expect, and when our expectations are not fulfilled, we suffer.

Everyone at the club had their own plans and agendas and were often two-faced; pleasant and agreeable to your face, but so willing to stab you in the back when it suited their plans. I was sad and depressed. I was always keeping up appearances on the surface, but inside, I was dying. I was not in love with Lenore, but I kept hanging on to the memory that I was. She had stopped coming home. She would claim she had to pull another all-nighter on her schoolwork, and I would believe her every time. I didn't want to believe the truth.

One night, I found myself in bed with Kelly, and soon after that, I came home from the club to find Lenore in bed with one of the guys from the upstairs apartment. When I found them, Lenore just smirked at me. She knew what time I would be getting home and had wanted me to find them. I think it was the only way she knew how to break up with me.

Shortly after this, she got the opportunity to study abroad, and she was gone. After seven years together on and off, it was finally over. The worst part of it was finding out that she had been hooking up with other people for pretty much our entire relationship. I had my suspicions, but had no idea how much she was actually cheating. I felt like an idiot. I felt like I couldn't trust my own judgment of character anymore. I'd always been self-confident, but not anymore. Lenore had shattered that.

Kelly wanted to get into a relationship, but I couldn't do it. I was too broken from what Lenore had done to me. Instead of finding comfort in Kelly, I used her as the target of my rage, and I treated her terribly. You won't hear me say the words, "I regret" very often, but I regret the way I treated Kelly. It wasn't right, and it wasn't fair. She didn't deserve it. Fortunately, ten years later, thanks to Facebook, I would get a chance to apologize for my actions.

With Lenore gone, we now had an open room in the apartment. I asked my friend Jack from school if he wanted to move in and pool our resources and talents to start a home recording studio. He jumped at the opportunity. Kelly and Jenny moved out. We had two open bedrooms, so I asked two other guys I had met in the clubs to move in. One was an aspiring DJ, and the other was a tech guy. Jack and I began packing my room full of synthesizers and recording equipment, and anything we didn't already have, I started buying on credit.

The four of us decided to turn our apartment into a business, and Symfonic Productions was born. I adopted the pseudonym Master Symfony and Jack made music under the name New Horned Messiahs. Jack had the best ears for sound engineering and was really good at creating beats, and I was a good composer of melody and harmony. Together, we started producing electronic music. We were Master Symfony and the New Horned Messiahs. I still think it was such a good name for a musical duo.

One of the things we did was collect vintage synthesizers. We would buy one off eBay, and Jack would make as many different sounds with it as he could to sample for later use. We would then sell the synthesizer, buy another one, and do the same thing. We quickly started to create a massive collection of sounds that no one else had.

We also started to record rock bands in the house. We would set up the band in the living room and put the singer in the shower for isolation and natural reverb. Then we would run the cables down the hall to my bedroom, which was now covered from floor to ceiling with all kinds of electronic equipment.

We made beats for aspiring hip hop artists, but none of this brought in much money. It was fun, but not profitable. To make money, we ran the video system at the club on the weekends, and, during the week, we worked as freelance audio-visual technicians for conventions and business meetings. Things went pretty well that way for a while, and then I got the idea for Ibiza.

Ibiza, if you don't know, is an island off the coast of Spain near the Rock of Gibraltar. It is home to some of the largest, grandest nightclubs in the world. I thought if I could convince one of these clubs to put in a video system like the one I had in Boston, then I could get us some global notoriety. Fortune favors the bold, right? Maybe, but it also crushes the naïve and under-prepared.

Ibiza is a summer resort destination, and I arrived right at the beginning of the season, before the party was in full swing, I remember sitting on the plane feeling very proud and full of myself. I was a young entrepreneur boldly branching out in the world! I was going to sell a system to one of these clubs, and there was no doubt in my mind. I was in for a rude awakening.

Sometimes in this life, a brief encounter with a total stranger can have a profound and lasting effect. To get to Ibiza, I had to fly from Boston to Iceland, from Iceland to Germany, and from Germany to Ibiza. On the first leg of this journey, I had an encounter like that.

Sitting next to me on the plane was a woman in her late

forties, maybe early fifties, who inquired about where I was going and what I was doing. As we chatted, I became increasingly restless and fidgety, and she asked me if I was feeling okay. I told her, "Yes, I just need a cigarette." It had been a while since I had gone an hour or two without a smoke, especially when I was sitting around doing nothing. The boredom was driving me crazy. This is what I will never forget. She explained how she used to smoke but had quit when she realized that what she was craving wasn't nicotine. What she was really craving was *air*.

"Have you noticed that when you smoke you take deep breaths?" she asked. Before I could answer, she continued, "I figured out that if I just took a few deep breaths, I didn't need a cigarette anymore. Try it." I was skeptical, but I closed my eyes and took a deep breath and let it out, and then another one, and another. then another.

When I opened my eyes, I still wanted a cigarette, but the restlessness had left my body. My hands and feet were still. I felt better. It didn't stop me from running to the nearest place to smoke when we landed, but the experience planted a seed somewhere deep in my memory.

After the three flights, I finally landed in Ibiza. I got my rental car, drove to my hotel, and crashed. The next day, I started driving around to the different clubs, trying to get a manager or an owner to talk to me. There was one problem. I didn't speak any Spanish, and everyone I tried to talk to didn't speak English, so I couldn't even get my foot in the door. I continued trying for weeks. The few times I did get someone to meet with me, they didn't really understand what I was trying to sell them, and so were not interested.

My second or third day there, I was walking down the street when a man approached me carrying a small black bag. He flipped open the bag to reveal a bunch of watches. He asked, "Hey man, you want to buy a Rolex?"

I said, "No thanks. I'm good, man."

He then flipped the watches back to reveal a compartment underneath, and, in a quieter voice, he asked if I wanted any cocaine, ecstasy, or hash. I laughed and asked him his name. He said his name was Robbie, and we shook hands. I said, "Look Robbie, back at home, I'm a dealer just like you, so I know the hustle." He smiled. "Here's the deal," I said. "If you give me a good deal right now, I will only buy from you, and I will buy a lot, because I am going to be here all summer. How much for ten E pills?"

He paused for a moment and then replied, "Fifty American."

I agreed, and we did the deal. It was more than double what I would have paid at home, but he had to make his money, and it was far cheaper than the twenty or thirty dollars apiece that other people would be paying in the clubs.

If you can get the drugs cheap enough, it is always easy to make fair-weather friends, even with a language barrier. If you start handing out free drugs to people, they are going to hang around to see if you will give them more. So I started going out to a different magical club every night, giving out drugs and partying with strangers.

There were all sorts of amazing clubs. There was one with a retractable roof, like a football stadium, and when the weather was fair, they would open the roof for open air dancing under the stars with a capacity of ten thousand.

My absolute favorite club experience though, was this place called El Paridiso. It had a Greco-Roman hedonist theme, and the main dance floor was a big, round affair surrounded by big columns covered in vines and flowers. The dance floor was recessed into the ground by three massive steps, and the DJ booth was positioned on a platform between two columns overlooking the whole scene. At the end of the night, the DJ would drop a house remix of Gene Kelly's Singing in the Rain, and jets of seawater, pumped in from the ocean outside, would spray out of the steps, rapidly filling the main dance floor with water. As the dance floor transformed into a chest-deep swimming pool, pandemonium would ensue. People would take their clothes off, girls would climb up on the shoulders of the guys, and packs of cigarettes and drugs would float by. And then, without warning, the song would end, the dance floor would drain, the house lights would come on, and that was the end of the night.

For weeks, I spent my nights partying and my days on the beach; eating, shopping, and sleeping. I gave up on working and just tried to have a good time. And I did, until I didn't. You can't take that much ecstasy for that long and not eventually run out of serotonin and fall into depression. My brain eventually fried, and man, when it hit me, it hit hard.

I decided to go home early. I packed up my stuff, checked out of the hotel, and drove my rental car back to the airport. However, when I tried to switch my tickets at the airport, I encountered some difficulty. I think I was short on funds or something. I can't quite remember the details, but what I do remember is having a breakdown at the airport. I didn't know who to call or what to do. I was stuck overseas, and all I wanted to do was go home.

I had failed at what I had set out to accomplish. I had partied too hard, and I was feeling quite broken. I called my parents and sobbed like a child. Somehow, I got my flights changed, boarded the plane, and headed back to the States. Everything was fine until I got to customs.

When I arrived back at Logan airport in Boston, I marched towards customs and immigration with everyone else. I approached the officer, removed my sunglasses and handed him my passport. I was wearing white linen pants, a white linen V-neck t-shirt, sandals, and silver jewelry. I looked strung out. I was probably about one hundred and twenty pounds, and you could count my ribs through my shirt.

He looked at my passport and then back at me and then asked if I had anything to declare. I hesitated for the briefest moment and then said, "No."

He took a deep breath, let it out and said, "I need to have a look in your bag."

I said, "Okay," trying to sound agreeable and not panic.

He opened my bag. At first glance, it looked normal. There were clothes and toiletries, but then he discovered the wooden box.

One of the things I had purchased in Ibiza was a water pipe. It was made of glass and came with an ornately carved, wooden carrying case. He pulled out the box and asked, "What's this?"

As calmly and casually as I could, I replied "It's a tobacco pipe." I felt pretty safe. I knew paraphernalia wasn't illegal, and I hadn't used the pipe.

"Tobacco pipe?" he asked and opened the box.

It was obviously a bong for smoking weed, but I stuck to my guns and said, "Yes."

He sniffed it and could tell it was unused. He closed the box and pointed at the lid, "What's this?" he asked, pointing to the engraving on the box of a giant marijuana leaf.

"A design of a leaf," I replied, getting frustrated.

"A leaf?" he responded, with a questioning tone. "I'm going to give you one more chance here. What kind of leaf?"

I just couldn't do it.

"A tobacco leaf," I said, reluctantly.

He closed my suitcase, picked it up and said, "Come with me please, sir."

You know, when a cop starts calling you sir, things are not going well. He led me into the back and put me in a tiny room with no windows and one door. It had a stainless steel table and four chairs, two on each side. He put my suitcase on the table and told me to have a seat. He closed the door and left. He returned a few minutes later with two more uniformed officers. Things were getting tense, and I was starting to sweat.

He sat down across from me with the two other officers standing behind him. He put both hands on my suitcase and spoke. "Here's the deal," he said. "I'm going to go through your entire suitcase with a fine-tooth comb. If there's anything else in here, I'm going to find it. Before I do, if you tell me the truth and show me what else is in here, I will be easy on you. However, if you make me find it, I will be as hard on you as I possibly can. So I'm going to ask you just this once. Is there anything else in here I should know about?"

I knew he was serious, and I had already tried to call this guy's bluff. I wasn't willing to push my luck, so I decided the best option was to tell the truth and face the consequences. I

grabbed a stuffed frog from the bag, handed it to him and said, "There are two grams of hash sewed up inside."

"Is that it? I'm not going to find anything else?" he asked.

I said, "Yes, that's it."

He then proceeded to empty out all of my belongings onto the table and go through them. When he didn't find anything else, he relaxed a little and thanked me for being honest.

Then it was time to search me, and he asked me to stand up and put my hands on the wall. Here I was in this tiny room with these three big customs agents and no cameras. These guys could have done anything to me, and no one would have known. You could cut the anxiety in the room with a knife. All I could think was, "How can I break the tension? Maybe if I can make these guys laugh, I might just get out of this."

He asked me to separate my feet, and I complied. Just before he patted me down, and in an apologetic tone, he said, "I'm going to have to get a little friendly with you, if you know what I mean." I saw my chance and took it. It was a gamble. It could have gone either way, but I went for it.

I looked over my shoulder at him and said, "You're not

the first guy to get that kind of friendly with me," and winked. Then I held my breath and waited there for half a second, where my heart stopped. He said nothing, and I thought I was screwed. But then he laughed a big belly laugh, and the two other officers laughed, and the whole mood shifted.

He finished searching me and didn't find anything else. "Here's what we're going to do," he said. "We're going to pretend like this doesn't exist," pointing to the stuffed frog. I nodded slowly. He then informed me that even though the bong was unused, it was apparently illegal to bring in paraphernalia from outside the country. He gave me the minimum fine for that offense, which was five hundred dollars.

He then proceeded to tell me that if I could pay that right now, I could be on my way. If not, he would have to lock me up until I could get someone to come down and pay the fine.

I held up my credit card and asked, "Do you take MasterCard?" I paid my fine and headed back to my apartment on Mission Hill. It was August, and it was hot in the city. Boston can be like a pressure cooker in the summer.

Chapter Nine

I was miserable and depressed. I felt like a failure. It was hot, and customs had stolen my hash, but I had made it back.

It was September 11th of 2001 at about nine in the morning when my phone rang. It was too early. I let it go to voicemail, but it rang again. Frustrated and wanting to sleep, I grabbed the phone to look at the caller ID. It was my mother. Why was my mom calling me so early in the morning? I put the phone down and rolled back over, but she called again. This time, I answered, and asked what she wanted, what was so important?

My mom said, "Turn on the TV."

"Why?" I asked, frustrated.

"Just turn on the TV," she insisted.

"Fine," I said, throwing off the covers and getting out of bed. I pulled on some pants and walked down the hall to the living room. "What channel?" I asked.

"Any channel," she replied. That seemed odd. Nothing is ever on every channel. I flipped on the TV, and there it was.

My mouth dropped open as I saw my first images of an airplane flying into the World Trade Center in New York City. Slowly, I managed to say, "Holy shit."

I don't think I had ever sworn in a conversation with my conservative Christian mother before that moment out of respect and fear of rebuke, but I said it, and her only reply was, "Yes."

We sat there in silence for a few minutes watching the images on the TV. Finally, I said, "I better go wake up my roommates and let them know what's going on." My mom replied, "Oh, honey, stay inside and be safe today, please." "Okay, Mom, I will," I said and hung up the phone.

I woke up my unhappy roommates, who had a similar reaction to my own when they saw what was going on on the TV. I had my computer rigged up to capture video off the TV to use in my videos for the club, so I immediately turned it on. I gathered footage from as many news channels as I could.

That weekend, no one came out to the club. No one wanted to gather in large groups, and after a couple of weeks with low numbers, they started making cutbacks. They needed a DJ, but not a VJ, so they let me go, and replaced me with a DVD player. My corporate gigs quickly dried up as everyone began canceling their conventions, and I found myself being crushed by the wheel of *saṃsāra* once again.

I had lost all legitimate sources of income. I had no serotonin left in my body from taking too much ecstasy, and I was horribly depressed. I was sitting on a mountain of debt from the recording studio, and from spending two months in Ibiza, and the girl with whom I'd spent seven years of my life was gone. Oh, and I forgot to mention that my cat Bump had stopped coming home. My life was starting to sound like a bad country music song.

I didn't want to fight. I didn't want to "soldier on". As far as I could see, life was mostly problems and pain, and happiness was fleeting. I had nothing to look forward to. I just wanted to give up, lay down, and die. Could I do that? Yes, I could, I thought. I decided to try and drink myself to death.

I went out and bought a bottle of Jack Daniels, and then another, and another. I spent weeks trying to kill myself with alcohol, like Nicholas Cage in Leaving Las Vegas. I would drink until I passed out. I'd wake up and think, "Not dead yet." Then I would drink until I passed out again. I had a poster on my wall of the opening monolog from the film Trainspotting. It goes like this:

"Choose Life. Choose a job. Choose a career. Choose a family. Choose a fucking big television, choose washing machines, cars, compact disc players, and electrical tin openers. Choose good health, low cholesterol, and dental insurance. Choose fixed interest mortgage repayments. Choose a starter home. Choose your friends. Choose leisurewear and matching luggage. Choose a three-piece suit on hire, purchase in a range of fucking fabrics. Choose DIY and wondering who the fuck you are on Sunday morning. Choose sitting on that couch watching mind-numbing, spirit-crushing game shows, stuffing fucking junk food into your mouth. Choose rotting away at the end of it all, pissing your last in a miserable home, nothing more than an embarrassment to the selfish, fucked up brats you spawned to replace yourselves. Choose your future. Choose life. But why would I want to do a thing like that? I chose not to choose life. I chose somethin' else."

I would lay there in my drunkenness, staring at these wonderful bits of writing by John Hodge and think, "This is what society expects from me. This is what I've been taught I should do. This is what will give me a life of fulfillment and happiness." But I couldn't do it. If that was a happy life, I would rather have been dead. I was with Renton. I chose not to choose life. I chose something else.

I had stopped going out. I wasn't answering my phone. Once, my brother showed up to check on me in his EMT uniform, and my roommates woke me up. "Yo, Jordan, the cops are here!" I jumped up and looked out the peephole and breathed a sigh of relief. "It's just my brother, guys, calm down. He's an EMT, not a cop."

I had been living in a drunken state for weeks, when one day, I was rudely woken up by someone poking me in the back. I rolled over to see Matthew nudging me with his shoe, like he was checking to see if I was dead.

He said, "Okay, so you are alive."

I barely replied, "What the hell are you doing here, man? What do you want?"

"I need your help," he said. "I have spinal meningitis."

I sat up, "What? What the hell is that? And how did you get it?" I looked on the floor for some pants.

"I was walking the dogs in the park, and I picked up a dead bird to keep the dogs from getting it. That's the only thing I can think of. I need to go to the hospital. I don't have anyone who can run the pizza shop that I'm managing. I trust you. I know you can do it. Can you help me out?" Matthew could have asked me for a kidney, and I would've given it to him. "Yes, of course," I said.

I don't think that Matthew planned on getting spinal

meningitis to get me off the couch, but I also know that there are no accidents or coincidences. And it's not about luck, either. Everything happens for a reason and has a purpose. This is not a universe of chaos, but one of most profound order. I credit Matthew with saving my life at that moment. If he hadn't shown up and asked for my help, I would have eventually succeeded in drinking myself to death. He gave me a reason to get up and start living again.

Over the years, I've come to appreciate these people the most; the people that come along and nudge you when you're stuck. It is a precious thing in life. Cherish those people who won't let you give up, who won't let you lay down and die. That is a special person.

I went down to the pizza shop, and Matthew gave me the rundown on the ins and outs of the business, and then he went to the hospital. After about ten days, he was well and came back to work. I stayed on as the assistant manager. It wasn't a hard job, and I could make extra cash on the side delivering the pizzas. I was using crystal meth a lot during this period, and to make my habit more affordable, I was selling it, too. The more you buy, the cheaper the price per unit. That's the way the drug game works.

I started buying it by the ounce. At the time, getting caught with one ounce of crystal meth could get you twenty-five years in prison. I was using the stuff all day, every day, and it made me edgy and paranoid. I wasn't just an angry kid acting out anymore. I was a grown man who was rapidly becoming a thug and a criminal. I didn't care about anyone or anything anymore. I just wanted to watch the world burn. I had only two possible destinations: death or jail.

I had accepted the likelihood of both or either when Angela came twirling into the pizza shop one day, and my life changed forever in a single moment. I didn't know it at the time, but that was the end of my childhood and the beginning of my adult life.

Chapter Ten

When I say that Angela twirled into my life, it's because she did just that. My very first memory of her is at the pizza shop. She had been the manager originally and had hired Matthew, and when she quit, Matthew became the manager. When he got sick, they hired me.

One day, Angela came by the shop with her girlfriend to get a pizza. I was behind the counter, and Matthew was outside smoking. He was chatting with them for a bit, and then Angela came in wearing knee-high leather boots, and a purple velvet shirt. Her blue hair was cut short and styled spiky. She had that big, bad-ass dragon tattoo on her upper arm. She looked at me, smiled, twirled around in a circle, and went and grabbed a soda from the cooler.

Honestly, I didn't think anything of our first meeting. I smiled back and went back to work. A couple of weeks later, unbeknownst to either of us, Matthew invited us both individually out for drinks. To hear her tell it, Angela thought Matthew was asking her out, but when he came to pick her up with his girlfriend in the car, she was confused. When they arrived at the restaurant, she saw me sitting there and realized that Matthew had a different plan. In Matthew's words, he just wanted to put us both in the same place to see what might happen.

We all had a nice dinner, and afterwards, we went back to my place to smoke some weed. After we smoked and hung out for a while, Matthew and his girl decided to leave. Angela stayed, and we hung out until about two a.m.

Angela said she needed to get going and had every intention of walking home. As far as cities go, Boston is a relatively safe one, but my neighborhood of Mission Hill was one of the rougher ones. I wasn't about to let her walk home alone in the middle of the night. She thought I was being silly but accepted a ride home.

I was really into her, but she was dating a woman. So I didn't think we would ever be more than friends, and that was okay with me. I had gone a year without dating anyone after Lenore. I felt like I had to get to a point where I could trust myself again.

A couple of days later, I asked Angela to join me for lunch, and after that, we started spending more and more time together. In our conversations, I learned that she had grown up in Texas. She had a view of the world unlike anyone I had ever met before, and I found it refreshing. After high school, she moved to Colorado where she had met a guy. When he decided to move east, she went with him, not because she liked him all that much, but because she wanted to check out Boston. When they broke up, she decided to stay, and, after living in her car briefly, moved in with a friend and was sleeping on the couch. When I met her, she had temporarily sworn off men, and was dating women.

The more we hung out, the more into her I got, but for weeks, nothing happened. I was too scared to make a move. I didn't think she was into me that way until one night when we were sitting on the couch, drinking beer and watching TV. I felt like I was in junior high. Her hand was so close to mine, and I wanted to grab, and to kiss her so badly. I thought to myself, "Just caress her hand a little, but do it in a way that you can play it off as an accident, if it's not received well." Nervously, cautiously, I brushed my hand against hers. A few tense moments passed while my heart slammed into my throat, and then she touched me back.

Yes! I slipped my hand into hers, and it felt so good. We sat there for a few moments, enjoying the feeling of our energies mingling in our fingers. It felt so right. It felt like I had found the other pole of my magnet. Then our arms were around each other, and we were kissing.

Bliss! Divine bliss flowed through me in a way I had never experienced. After that, we were inseparable. I thought about her all the time. Nothing else mattered. She was all I wanted.

Despite our strong connection, we were both hesitant to start a new relationship. Our recent relationships had ended badly, and we believed that relationships were the problem, not the people in them. The belief was that relationships start off good and end up bad, but this reality that we had created was out of alignment with the Truth.

When something is True, that means it's running straight. If we are in alignment with what is True, then our reality is also True. It is running straight. If our reality is out of sync with what is True, then it is no longer running straight, and this wobble causes internal friction. We begin operating and making choices based upon false pretenses, and we project our inner conflicts out into the world.

The only way we can change the world is to go into

ourselves and resolve our own inner problems. As long as we continue to project our problems and insecurities out into the world, there will be poverty, injustice, inequality, and conflict. The world doesn't have problems. We have problems, and we blame the world for them.

After having multiple relationships that ended badly, Angela and I used thought to draw a conclusion. The conclusion was that relationships are bad. We based the conclusion on our past experiences. Was the conclusion True? No. Why? Because we made the conclusion based upon limited information.

Some relationships are bad, but some are great and incredibly beneficial to both parties involved. Angela and I have a relationship like that now, but at that time, we had never experienced one before. We believed that relationships equaled pain, and we had a desire to avoid that pain in the future. If we had given that belief power, and acted on it, then we would have denied ourselves the love that we have shared for the last eighteen years.

Humans do this all the time in a million different ways. Here's another common example. A woman breaks a man's heart. He gets back out there and dates a different woman. This woman breaks his heart too. He decides to try again. He meets a new woman, but in the end, she breaks his heart as well. The man draws a conclusion: All women will break my heart.

Is that True? No.

The Truth is that three women hurt the man, but the man decides that there is no one out there for him. He believes that there is no love in this life for him. He makes a decision and takes action on a false conclusion. He lives alone, and does not date, and these actions make him unhappy and unfulfilled. His distorted reality leads to a great deal of suffering.

Take a moment and consider how many false conclusions are affecting your decisions and actions every moment of every day. For Angela and me, it wasn't long before the distortions we had about relationships faded away, and love took hold. Love is strong. Once it's got you, you can resist all you want, but love always wins.

Before long, we were exclusively together. We had some rules. Number one was no fighting. Eighteen years later, we have still never had a fight. We disagree for sure, but we don't fight. I have always said to her, "I just want you to do what you want and be happy. I'm glad that involves me now, but if that ever changes, that's okay, too. What's most important is that you do what makes you happy, and that our relationship supports that."

I was at my absolute worst when Angela came along. It was as if I forgot that there was anything good, true, or kind inside of me. I was barely a human being. I had reverted back to animal nature. I'd become so hard in every way. My heart felt like stone. But Angela saw past all that. She looked at me like I was the greatest man she had ever met, and that felt good. She saw something that I couldn't, and all I knew was that I wanted to live up to that look. I wanted to be the man she thought I was; I didn't want to let her down. I was going to be better. I can tell you the exact moment I made that choice.

Angela had tickets to a David Bowie concert. She is a big fan of his music. I like his music well enough, but I've never been a true fan. She wanted me to go to the concert with her, and I was happy to go. I had brought the last of my crystal meth with me because I didn't go anywhere at this point without it. I needed to pick up more. I was down to only a couple days' supply. Looking back on this now, part of me wonders if that was a little divine intervention.

On the way to the show, I was snorting meth in the car, so Angela knew I had it on me. We parked the car and started walking towards the entrance to the venue. We were standing in line approaching security, and Angela was getting nervous. She was worried about me getting busted by security.

I wanted to say to her, "Do you know how many times I've smuggled drugs? I've crossed international borders carrying drugs! I got caught by US Customs and didn't even get busted. I got off with a fine, I am not concerned about these rent-a-cops catching me."

But I didn't say any of that. Something else in my head said, "Look at how uncomfortable you are making her. Do you really want to make her feel this way?" The answer was a clear no. I didn't want to do anything that would cause her discomfort. I wanted to make her laugh and smile. I wanted to make her happy. I thought, "You've got her and the music. You don't need the drugs."

The two monkeys inside my head, the happy monkey and the angry monkey, fought each other all the way to the trash barrel, where the happy monkey won the battle. I threw the last of my drugs in the trash.

Dumbfounded, I walked back to Angela and looked at her happy, relieved, smiling face and said, "I can't believe I just threw drugs away for you."

Drugs were more important than anything to me for a

very long time, and just like that, they weren't. Apparently, I had found a better drug: love. It was a wonderful night. It was an outdoor amphitheater, we were so happy, and so in love, and Bowie sang wonderfully under the stars.

Angela became my drug. She took the number one slot in my life, and everything else was secondary to being the best man and partner I could be for her.

What happened in that moment before I threw the drugs in the trash? What was that pause? Mindfulness has become a very popular concept in the last ten years or so, but what do we mean by mindfulness? Is it something we can practice and cultivate and strengthen? Is it something that can happen spontaneously, without warning? Mindfulness is kind of funny.

The word describes what it is: mind-ful-ness. I think it's the full part that's confusing, because the experience of it seems like the opposite. It feels like an emptying of the mind, or at least a pushing aside of everything for a moment to find an empty space. Mind space might be a better way of describing it. Mindfulness is a pause in time, and that time is the space between stimulus and response.

Most of us go through life mainly reacting to stimulation; doing exactly what the word reacting implies. We repeat the same actions over and over again. Stimulus comes through the senses; what we see, touch, taste, hear, and smell, and then our brain tallies up all that information and compares it to memory. Memory is a record of all our previous sensory experiences, plus our preferences. Was it pleasurable or painful?

If we take action in the present based upon a memory of pleasure or pain from the past, then we are reacting to the situation. We just automatically act, and it all happens so fast. We don't even understand it. We just think "this is me."

When Angela and I were standing in line to get into the concert, the stimuli were the illegal drugs I was carrying and the security guards searching people for drugs. In reaction to these stimuli, Angela's brain created an equation instantly: drugs + authority = trouble, jail, punishment, pain. This memory of pain, projected into the future, caused fear in Angela. My brain created a different equation: drugs + security = a joke. My memory of pleasure projected into the future, created hope in me. Two different people exposed to the same stimuli created two completely different reactions.

But there was another factor that my brain could not ignore; my love for Angela. My desire to avoid causing her pain forced me to pause. That pause is mindfulness. Mindfulness creates a space, a moment where a person gets to decide to take action based on memory (System 1), or choose a different response based upon higher cognitive reasoning (System 2).

Mindfulness is the space between stimulus and response. Response is the key word here. A reaction is an automatic, mindless action. A response is a conscious choice based upon reflection of the past and the present situation. Now, to be clear, one might consciously choose to do what they've always done, but it would still be a response, not a reaction, because System 2 was used.

System 2 is like a muscle. If we exercise it often, it becomes strong. We can practice mindfulness, and the more we do, the more easily we will respond to the events of our lives. Reacting leads to suffering.

Consider a time when someone at work or at home asked you something that required you to make a decision, but you were distracted by some other task that was already occupying your attention. System 1 kicks into gear. Very quickly in this situation, your memory decides what answer will lead to pain, and what answer will lead to pleasure, and without mindfulness, you react, perhaps harshly or aggressively.

A few moments pass, and System 2 kicks in, and you reflect on what has transpired. You feel wrong or guilty for the actions you have taken, and apologize for your behavior. What do we commonly say? "I'm sorry for how I reacted," or something similar.

At the concert with Angela, there was a pause that occurred before I threw my drugs away. I had an insight; an epiphany. That is the power of mindfulness. Insight is not a product of thought. One does not come to an insight by sitting and thinking. One has an insight in the absence of the movement of thought. When thought pauses and space opens in the mind, insight can enter into that space. Insight is when we receive a direct message from the collective consciousness.

Insight comes from the collection of all human experience. No pre-existing knowledge is required to receive and understand an insight, because pure consciousness is unaffected by the individual ego. It is always aligned to the Truth. The insight acts on the individual, correcting any distortion in their reality and realigning it to the Truth. Albert Einstein famously said, "I think ninety-nine times and find nothing. I stop thinking, swim in silence, and the Truth comes to me."

An epiphany happens in a flash. It just comes to you. An instant download of knowledge from the Universe. The epiphany that I had that night at the Bowie concert was that I didn't need the drugs. I had Angela and the music; my two loves. As I continued to think about that Truth, I realized that the drugs hadn't given me that feeling of connectedness in a long time. Every time I would take more or try to go for longer, I was hoping it would plug me back into everything again, but it never did. I was chasing a memory of pleasure doing the same thing over and over again, expecting different results.

This re-writing of my reality back to what was True marked the end of my use of hard drugs and psychedelics. I didn't go to rehab. I didn't enter a twelve-step program. I saw the Truth, and it acted on me. Like sticking your hand in a fire and getting burned. Once you've been burned, you just can't do it again.

I didn't like the Truth. I wanted to believe drugs would work again, but it doesn't matter whether we like it or not. It does not matter what we believe. The Truth just is. We can either align to it or fight it and suffer. You've heard the famous saying, "Pain is inevitable, but suffering is optional." If you have a physical body, you will experience pain. There's no way around it. Liberation will not save us from the pain of a broken leg. If we break a leg, we will feel pain. If in that physical pain, we say to ourselves "this shouldn't have happened. I didn't do anything to deserve this broken leg. This is not fair!" that is suffering. Fighting against what *is* is a choice.

Unfortunately, it's most often an unconscious choice.

There Is No Me

It is every individual's right to choose to suffer, or to choose to wake up from the delusion of belief and look at the Truth. You get to decide.

After the concert, I locked myself in my room for a few days, sweated and detoxed. I came out, showered, ate some food, and decided I needed to stop messing around with the pizza shop and find a job that would hopefully lead to a career. I got a job as a bank teller. I went from a thug in a sleeveless shirt with tattoos, to a banker in a suit and tie. Because of Angela and my love for her, my whole perspective on that quote from the opening monologue of Trainspotting had shifted. Now I felt like Renton at the end of the film. I was choosing a job, a career, and maybe even a family. I wanted the big television, washing machine, and mortgage repayments; I wanted all of it. I was choosing life.

When I threw my meth in the trash, it was all I owned at the time. One could say it was good luck, or give it providence by calling it divine intervention, or dismiss it as coincidence, but it was very unusual for me at that time to be so low on supply. If there had been a bag waiting for me when I got home, maybe things would have been different, but there wasn't.

What we call luck is just a conclusion we make based on desire. If we like what happens we say it is good luck. If we don't like it, we say it was bad luck. Things are not good or bad. Change is just happening. For everything we think is bad, something good comes. And for every good thing, a cost is paid. Things are as they are, regardless of what we think about them. Everything is divine.

Divine is the good and the bad, the dark and the light, the up and the down, the inner and the outer, the subject and the object, the thinker and the thought; all is one in a myriad of forms. So where exactly would the divine intervene? Everything is working toward one goal so vastly beyond one's individual perspective, one cannot know it.

So, to dismiss something as mere coincidence dismisses all of the power and grandness of this fact. God, the Universe, the Force, whatever you want to call it is not for you or against you. We are not pieces of it. We are it. And so everything that happens—good or ill—is happening from our own doing. Everything is always exactly as it should be, regardless of our preferences.

Chapter Eleven

It was September again, and two of my roommates were moving out and moving on with their lives. Jack and I decided to downsize to a two-bedroom apartment in the Brighton neighborhood of Boston. I didn't like the fact that Angela was still living at her friend's place with no actual bedroom, so, after only knowing each other for three months, I asked her to move in with me.

I was working at the bank from nine to five, and Angela was working third shift at a bakery from eleven p.m. to seven a.m. She would arrive home in the morning when I was leaving, sleep while I was at work, and then we would have a few hours together in the evening. It wasn't the best, but it didn't matter. We were so infatuated with each other. We made the most of the little time we saw each other each day.

I hope you have experienced new love in your life. It truly is one of the best things life has to offer. Like Kenny Loggins sang, "Even though we ain't got money, I'm so in love with you, honey." Or Sonny and Cher's "I got you. You got me. I got you to hold my hand. I got you to understand. I got you to walk with me. I got you to talk with me. I got you to kiss goodnight. I got you to hold me tight. I got you. I won't let go. I got you to love me so." Music

Jordan P. Lashley

captures the emotion of love so well, and love is so powerful that it's easy to do. That's why so many love songs exist, and why anyone who has experienced love can relate to them.

But what is love? Is it just an emotion in human beings, or is it more than that? One thing I think we can all agree on is that love is unconditional. Every "thing" that exists, exists under conditions. So we can logically conclude that love is not a thing. So what is it then? Love is energy. It is a force that acts, like gravity or inertia or Truth.

My whole life dissolved into Angela at that point. Everything I wanted to do involved her, and, when I wasn't with her, she was all I thought about.

One day while I was working at the bank, diligently taking one customer after another, I looked up from the cash drawer to the face of a smiling young man about my age, wearing a baseball cap and a button up shirt, nothing suspicious or out of the ordinary.

I said, "Hello," and he replied, "I guess you're the lucky one."

He slid a note across the counter to me. I was confused until I looked down and read it. It said something to the effect of: This is a robbery. I have a gun. Don't make a scene. Don't hit the alarm. Give me all the large bills, and I will leave quietly.

Bank policy was very clear on what we should do in the event of a robbery. Stay calm, give them what they want, and get them out of the bank as fast as possible. They did not require us to give them the dye pack, but they encouraged us to do it if we felt safe enough.

For those of you who don't know what the dye pack

is, it's a device that looks like a regular bundle of bills, but in the middle is a small explosive package of red dye. It works sort of like an invisible fence for a dog. When the bank robber leaves the bank, he crosses an invisible line that triggers the device. About thirty seconds later, it explodes, covering all of the money in red dye and making it unusable.

I finished reading the note and looked back up at his smug, smiling face. My first thought was, "If I reached through the hole and grabbed him by the shirt and pulled really hard, I bet I could smash his face into the glass hard enough to knock him out." We were expressly forbidden to interfere with a robbery in any way. They drilled that into us in training and told us we would be fired if we did so.

Remembering this fact, my next thought was, "Well, you're definitely getting the dye pack, you piece of shit. I pulled two stacks of real bills and sandwiched the dye pack in-between them and handed all of it over. I quickly handed him three more, so he was forced to put the first three into the bag without examining them closely. I handed him the rest and said, "That's it. I'm empty. Have a nice day, sir." I was never scared or worried for anyone else's safety. I never saw the gun. I doubt he even had one, but even if he had, I could tell he wasn't going to use it.

Following protocol to the letter, I waited until he exited the bank. I then calmly walked down the row of tellers to the supervisor, a little Puerto Rican lady in her fifties. I told her I had been robbed, that the robber had left the bank, and that we had to go lock the doors and call the police. "Are, are you serious?!" she stuttered. "Yes, deadly," I replied, chuckling at her reaction a little.

Flustered, she went and locked the door, informed the

manager, and the police were called to the bank. They eventually rewarded me with two hundred dollars for giving him the dye pack. I had saved the bank thousands, and all they gave me was two hundred dollars.

Banks are stingy unless you make it to upper management, and that would have taken years. I went to the cafe across the street after work that day, as I did on most days. They knew me and knew that I worked at the bank.

They asked me, "Hey, what happened at the bank today?"

"I got robbed," I replied.

"We thought so when we saw some guy running down the street with a smoking bag!" That made me laugh so hard. I wish I could have seen that, and the look on his face.

The managers liked me. The bankers trusted me. It wasn't a hard job physically or mentally, but it was boring. It was spirit-crushing work, eight hours a day, five days a week filled with repetition and monotony. When a fellow teller told me that they had only received a twenty-five-cent increase in pay after their review, I was done. Twenty-five cents. "That's it? That's kind of insulting. That's only ten bucks a week," I thought.

That's when I started thinking about enlisting in the military. The bank had potential for growth, but it was too slow. I wanted to advance faster. I started thinking the Air Force might be a good choice. I was off hard drugs. I was choosing life, right? Why not go into the military, get some electronics training, and see where it leads?

I remember thinking, "I wonder if I could go through basic training and play the good soldier game?" I thought I could. I thought I was hard. Oh, the arrogance of youth.

Then I started thinking of Angela. I thought, "There's no way I can leave her behind and go into the military."

You can't take your girlfriend with you if you enlist, but you can take your wife. I wondered if she would say yes if I asked her. I wondered and thought and agonized for days about it. I wish I had a super romantic story to tell you about how I proposed to Angela, but I don't.

One night, we were walking back from the liquor store to our apartment, chatting and carrying beer. I was talking about joining the Air Force, and I believe my exact words were, "What would you say if I asked you to marry me?" She stopped, turned, looked me in the eye, and asked, "Jordan, are you asking me to marry you?" Feeling shy and awkward, I said, "Well, yes. I suppose I am." She said, "Yes! Yes, I will marry you." And that was it.

Just like that, we were getting hitched. She had not met my family yet, nor I hers, but we set the date for March 21st, the vernal equinox. I brought Angela to Thanksgiving that year and introduced her to my family, and, at the end of the meal, informed them of our plan to get married in March. They were surprised, but supportive. My brother put his hands on Angela's shoulders and said, "Welcome to the family." I flew down to Texas later that year to meet Angela's family.

Neither of us wanted to get married in a church or a courthouse. We flirted with the idea of getting married in Las Vegas. I was partial to an Elvis wedding.

"Do you take this hunk-a-hunk of burning love to be your man?"

"Yes."

"Do you take this pretty mamma to be your wife?"

"Yes."

You know, that kind of thing. Angela's mom was having none of that, which I could understand. I found out that anyone could perform a marriage ceremony in Massachusetts. All we had to do was apply for a special permit with the governor's office. We wanted the wedding to be very small, with just my parents and hers; no grandparents, siblings, or extended family or friends.

Matthew and his girlfriend served as best man and maid of honor. Angela had been picking up extra cash working as a nanny for a young couple who allowed us to use their condo in Brookline for the ceremony. The father of the child Angela had been nannying, an English bloke, presided. I rented a tux. Angela bought a dress. The whole ceremony was quick, but lovely and magical. We all went out to dinner at The Prudential Center afterwards, and Angela and I spent the night in a fancy hotel down at the Seaport in Boston.

I had never made such a big decision so fast or so effortlessly before. What else can I say; when it's right, it's right. Angela and I met, started dating, moved in together, and got married, all within the span of eight months. I bet our families thought we would last six months, tops, but eighteen years later, we are still together and very much in love.

The idea that motivated me into marriage never actually happened. I never went into the Air Force. During my enlistment process, I failed a drug test for marijuana. I thought I had quit for long enough, but I guess not, and after that, the Air Force didn't want me.

I still wanted to quit the bank. We had received some

money from friends and family for the wedding and were deciding what to do next. We wanted a change, and Angela wanted to move back closer to her mom in Texas. We both made a list of the top three places we would want to live if we had the chance and showed them to each other. New Orleans, Louisiana was on both lists.

We both had a fantasy. A Hollywood idealized idea of New Orleans from vampire books and movies. We wanted to live an unconventional lifestyle, and the Big Easy seemed like a good place to do it. We quit our jobs, said goodbye to our friends and my family, and packed my big blue Dodge cargo van to the ceiling with all of our stuff and Angela's crazy cat, Yoshi. Towing Angela's Saturn behind us, we said goodbye to Boston and started driving toward my grandparent's house in Pennsylvania.

Our first day on the road was smooth sailing. Toward the end of the first day, I took a wrong exit and got a little turned around, which is not the easiest thing to do in a giant cargo van with another car in tow, but we managed well enough and arrived at my grandparents' place in one piece. The next morning, after saying goodbye to my grandparents, we headed towards West Virginia.

Driving through the foothills of the Appalachian Mountains is beautiful country. The highway goes up and down massive hills. It was raining, and we were heavily loaded down with a car in tow. I remember it was very stressful driving until we made it to Western Kentucky, where the landscape started to flatten out more.

We stopped for the night just outside of Memphis, Tennessee.

The next morning, we headed across the vast

nothingness of Arkansas. We arrived at Angela's mother's home in Fort Worth, Texas in the late afternoon. Three days alone in the car driving halfway across the country may have been perilous for many newlywed couples, but Angela and I have always been a good team. We have very different ways of viewing things that complement each other nicely, and it was a pleasant journey. We were enjoying being together on the adventure of life.

After a couple of days of visiting with Angela's family, we decided it was time to make the last leg of the journey from Texas to Louisiana.

The drive into New Orleans was a strange experience. After Baton Rouge, there's almost no solid land. It's all swamp and marshland. The highways are all on stilts because the whole city of New Orleans sits below sea level. We finally arrived, crossing the massive bridge over Lake Pontchartrain, which would become famous a year later when Hurricane Katrina would devastate the city.

That whole summer, we witnessed firsthand the flooding of the streets that happens every time it rains. We were told that there are massive pumping stations that can move about two inches of water per hour out to sea, but when it comes down hard and quick, as it usually does, it backs up into the streets. The futility of trying to keep the city amazes me to this day. It's a losing battle with much cost and hardship, and yet people persist.

We do that in so many ways. Once we have invested in something, a city, an idea, a belief, or a relationship, we refuse to let it go, because we are afraid that what comes next may not be as good as what we have now. Even if what we have now, we don't like very much.

We had booked a hotel near the French Quarter to stay in while we searched for an apartment. We checked in and then headed out to the famous Bourbon Street to explore. As we walked down the street, our first impression was not a good one. The Hollywood version of New Orleans is much cleaner. New Orleans, at least back then, was a dirty, dingy place. I don't know if it was because of the constant flooding or the constant partying, or the combination of the two, but the city smelled of vomit and urine. It was also the most racist place I had ever been. It was fairly equal in terms of population, with African American and Caucasians each making up about thirty-three percent of the population, but the Black population didn't want to have anything to do with the Whites, and the Whites didn't associate with the Blacks. They lived together but avoided each other. It was like segregation by choice.

I've never understood racism. It makes me feel awful, and it is very unpleasant to be around. It was everywhere in the culture there. Angela and I experienced it on our very first stroll down the street. We were not communicating verbally, but with a series of glances and facial expressions, we were thinking, "Are we in a bad part of town?" We would soon learn that it was like that everywhere.

We had just given up everything to move there. I don't think either one of us wanted to say we had made a huge mistake, so we tried to remain optimistic.

As we started our apartment search the next day, we were immediately struck by how inexpensive apartments were compared to Boston. We could get a one bedroom with a kitchen, living room, loft, washer & dryer, swimming pool, and a hot tub in a gated community for about a third of what we were spending on our tiny apartment in Brighton. We signed a year lease on a place in Gretna on New Orleans West Bank and paid six months' rent upfront. Now we just needed to find jobs, and we would be all set.

We found out why the cost of living was so low very quickly. The economy was horrible. There were no jobs to be found anywhere. There had always been work in Massachusetts. A few applications, a couple of interviews, and within a week, I was always able to find full-time work with reasonable pay and benefits. The bulk of the economy in New Orleans is in tourism, and it was the off season, and none of the restaurants and bars were hiring. I was so desperate for a job that I applied to places that I never would have in Massachusetts, like Walmart and McDonald's, but I couldn't even get hired there. It was depressing to lower my standards and still get rejected.

I think a big part of the problem was that I was a young white guy with a shaved head and tattoos. In Boston, this made me a punk rocker. In New Orleans, I was labeled a skinhead, racist Nazi. I know what it feels like to be profiled by the police. I know how it feels to be judged by your appearance and not by the content of your character. I see you. I feel you. It's terrible to live with that feeling.

We had a place to live and some money left for food, but our funds were rapidly dwindling. Angela picked up an internship at a tattoo shop, which brought in a little cash, but it also put her in some not so safe positions, like handing out flyers alone on Bourbon Street late at night. I would go stand with her sometimes, and we would nurse cheap beer and people watch. If you want to see how low humanity can go, Bourbon Street is a good place to see it.

We saw a businessman in his thirties or forties with a blue button-down shirt, tie, and khakis with boat shoes sloshing down the street one night. We watched in confusion as he approached a trashcan and began digging around in it. Had he dropped his cell phone in there? "What do you think he's looking for?" I asked Angela. She shrugged, and then we both watched in horror as he found it; a two-thirds empty beer. I am sure he was a fine, upstanding American during the day, but at night, blackout drunk, he was drinking trashcan beers. That was New Orleans.

I was running out of options for potential employment and spending more and more time sitting around the apartment, eating too much, drinking too much, and putting on weight. Sitting around in internet chat rooms and watching TV. At the end of our street in a strip mall was an Army recruitment office.

One day, coming from yet another failed job interview, depressed and fat and out of options, I decided to stop in. The Air Force didn't want me, but maybe the Army would take me. I hadn't smoked any weed in months at this point. So, I walked in and sat down with the Army recruiter.

I asked him flat out. "I tried to enlist in the Air Force but failed the drug test. Can I enlist in the army? I'm clean now." He said, "Yes, we can work around that." They told me to come back the next day for a physical and drug test. I went home and told Angela the good news.

I passed all the physical and mental examinations and was presented with my options for jobs within the Army. I chose to be a Patriot missile repair technician. I figured this would give me some good electronics training that I could build on. Once I had served long enough to qualify for the GI bill, then I could go to night school for electronics repair, or maybe engineering.

I thought this job would get me stationed on a base somewhere, and hopefully keep me away from the front lines. I was an angry guy, and I had been in plenty of stupid fistfights, but I was not interested in shooting anyone. With Angela in my life, I didn't relish the idea of being shot at myself, either. After all, this was all about choosing life, right?

I had a month before I was to ship off to basic training. Basic training would take three months, and that would be followed by six months of training in Patriot missiles. We needed to come up with a plan. I would be away from Angela for the better part of a year, and neither one of us liked the idea of her staying in New Orleans alone.

When I was in high school, my father spent his weekends converting the basement of our split-level ranch into a completely separate apartment in case my grandparents needed to live there at some point. I knew the apartment was sitting there empty, so I called my parents, explained the situation and asked if Angela could live with them until I got stationed somewhere. My parents agreed, and Angela liked this option, so we packed up the van and hit the road back to Massachusetts.

Chapter Twelve

Back in Massachusetts, I had a few weeks before I was to leave for basic training. I needed to get Angela settled in and get myself into better shape. I started running every day, something I hadn't done since I was about twelve. I had so enjoyed running back then. It got me out of the house, and I loved the feeling of independence it gave me. Running now felt just as good. Splitting wood felt good too. I split and stacked about four cords of wood, which gave me time to think.

Moving back into my parents' house after all this time was humbling. This whole "choosing life" thing was proving to be a lot harder than I had anticipated. I was processing a lot subconsciously, and I remember one day having a sudden realization that seemed to come out of nowhere. I suddenly had a newfound appreciation for everything my parents had accomplished.

For the first time, I saw my parents not as my parents, but as human beings themselves. I saw them not as this all-knowing authority, but as people like me, with desires, hopes, and fears, who didn't always know what they were doing, but who were trying their best. And yes, I saw them as human beings who sometimes made mistakes. But there are no mistakes. That's just a perception. Everything happens the way it's supposed to.

Then I began to think of all the horrible things I had said to them over the years. All of the stuff I had put them through, and how many problems I had caused in their existence. For the first time, I thought about all these things from their perspective and how they must have felt, and I felt the need to sit them down and apologize.

"I don't know how else to say it, so I'll just say it. I'm sorry for all I've put you through over the years," I said.

They looked at each other and then back at me. "We appreciate that son, but what has brought this on?" my father asked.

"I don't know, really," I said. "I've been doing a lot of reflecting, and I just started thinking about you guys as humans; not as my parents, just humans. It has given me a whole new perspective, and I just thought I would apologize." And that was it.

My ship-out date finally arrived. My bags were packed, and I was ready to go. The recruiter picked me up and drove me to the processing center. I sat and waited for the longest time. Hours went by, and finally someone came out and said, "Jordan?"

"Yes, sir," I replied.

"Come with me. We have a bit of an issue."

"Great. What now?" I thought.

They led me to a desk and told me to have a seat and explained that someone had made a mistake. They informed me that they could not give me the job working on the Patriot missiles, because I had failed the drug test when I tried to enlist in the Air Force.

"But I told the recruiter about that, and I've tested clean every time since," I protested.

"Yes, we know, but any failed drug test disqualifies you from the position," he informed me. "The only jobs we have shipping out today are EMS or tank driver. Which one do you want?"

So many thoughts ran furiously through my head. "So I can pull bullets out of people or have bullets shot at me? Was this the first test to see if I will fall in line and be a good soldier? I've already told everyone I'm going. I have to go. My whole future depends on this, but I really don't like either of these options, I don't know what to do!"

Finally, I asked to use the restroom, and I went and called my dad.

"What should I do, Dad?"

"Come home, son. Just walk away. If they are changing your job, then your enlistment contract is void. Tell them you're out and to bring you home," he said.

"But what else am I going to do? I'm so confused."

"Just come home. We can figure it out then. It's okay."

I broke down and wept. "Okay," I said, "I'll come home."

I cleaned myself up and went back to the office and told them I was out, and they took me home. I was crushed. I felt like such a failure. Twice now, I had tried the same path and failed. I was not meant to be a soldier. The universe had another purpose for me. I just couldn't see that yet.

I always refer to the next three years as purgatory, because it was the darkest period of my life. Not because anything was going badly for me, but because I was in darkness. I couldn't see anything clearly. I was lost and confused.

"On my way. Don't know where I'm going, but I'm on my way. Taking my time, but I don't know where." –Paul Simon.

I believed that the reason for all the drama in my life up to that point was being caused by interacting with too many people. I decided to limit my interactions with others as much as possible; family and work only. I thought that I had found the answer and that my luck was shifting when I took a relatively solitary, entry level position at a local company that manufactured trombones. But remember, there is no such thing as luck.

I was hired to work in the buffing room, which meant I would be polishing all of the brass and nickel parts, as well as the fully assembled instruments. This would prove to be the harshest environment I have ever worked in. How can I describe this to you? Picture a motor on a pedestal mounted to the floor. On each side is an axle that spins at approximately sixty-five miles per hour. At the end of the axle, we would attach various wheels made of different fabrics; some very stiff and rigid, some soft and fluffy, some in between, some large, some small. Imagine trying to grind a three-foot-long metal tube against the back tire of your car at high speed.

It was incredibly hard work; physically demanding and dangerous. The wheel was always trying to steal whatever I was working on out of my hands. A moment of distraction, and you could lose a finger, or worse. The polishing compounds we used would blow off the wheel and all over us. We had to wear goggles, face masks and earplugs. At the end of the day, we looked like coal miners, covered from head to toe, in every crack and crevice, with black or red dust, depending on which compound we were using that day. I did this for the next three years, twelve hours a day, from five a.m. to six p.m., six days a week, Monday through Saturday.

All I did was work, eat, and sleep. I didn't go out. I didn't have any friends. I completely forgot who I was, and life had no real purpose. I was just existing. My first day in the buffing room was terrible. It took months to get good at it and even longer to master it, but eventually, I was very good and became the buffing room supervisor. I kept working, hoping that eventually I would get promoted out of the buffing room and out onto the shop floor, making the instruments.

As the supervisor, I was brutal and ruthless. I drove my underlings hard and myself even harder. I was not a nice person to be around, but nobody in that place was. If you couldn't handle it, then you could get the fuck out.

I always wanted to be married and have a partner I could count on and go on adventures with. Children were never in my plan. I liked children, I just knew how much work they are. When I was about thirteen, my parents became foster parents for the state, and I did a lot of babysitting. I even worked in the nursery at my parent's church, so I knew first-hand the level of responsibility required to care for children.

I also was—and still am—of the opinion that there are too many humans on the earth. It's creaking under the strain of us all. I don't think anyone should be able to tell you how many children to have, but I do think some of us, for the good of all, should choose not to reproduce. But I would often say that if I had an opportunity to adopt, I would. If a child was coming anyway, I would do everything I could to help them. Just like I would for anyone else.

Being of these convictions, I decided to get a vasectomy so that Angela could stop taking birth control. The day before my procedure, we found out that Angela had the early stages of cervical cancer. The doctors said that if we wanted to have children, then we needed to do it soon. We had already decided not to have children, and the thought of a complicated pregnancy and a difficult birth that could take Angela from me and leave me alone with a child was not something I wanted to experience. It was an easy decision at the time. Angela would have a hysterectomy.

I remember being worried and anxious, and then relieved that she had survived the surgery and was recovering well. I remember bringing her flowers covered in buffing compounds from work. Angela's mother came up from Texas to help take care of her, and after a few days at the hospital, we brought her home. I was nervous and anxious. It was obvious that she was in a lot of pain, even with the medication.

I didn't know what to do or how to care for her, and

when I'm in an uncomfortable situation, I tend to default to humor. Everyone feels better after they've laughed, so I tried to make a joke. It was stupid and insensitive and would be one of the biggest mistakes I've made in our marriage. But there are no mistakes. Remember when I said all I wanted to do was live up to the way Angela looked at me? Well, this is where I disappointed her. She took me seriously, and with that one stupid sentence, I hurt her. She did not laugh. And I said, "Not funny?" And she said, "No, not funny."

I thought that was it and moved on, but somewhere inside, I had wounded her. Emotional wounds are just like physical wounds. If a physical wound goes untreated, it becomes infected. And if the infection goes unchecked, it will fester. An emotional wound, if left unchecked, will become anger, and if that anger goes unchecked, it will become hatred.

It would take a few years before this wound I had caused would show its effects. Angela is like a changeling. I've experienced many incarnations of my wife in our life together. Some versions I like better than others, but they're all her. And I love her with all my heart and soul.

After months of lying in bed, recovering from surgery and a bout of depression, Angela had put on some weight. She was not happy about this and decided she wanted to start going to the gym. She asked me if I would go with her. Now, I had never really been into physical fitness. I didn't play sports in high school, had always been thin, and had never had an interest in bodybuilding. I had worked out a little during the summer I had spent in Nashville with my brother, but that was about it, and besides, that had been my brother's thing. I was an artist. But I would support Angela in anything she wanted, so I said, "Sure, baby, I'll go to the gym with you." I had no idea at the time that this would be one of the most important decisions of my life.

Just like all the other really important decisions in my life, it was made effortlessly in the moment, without any conflict. At this point, Angela was working as the receptionist at the trombone factory, and we would head to the gym after work. She would go do cardio, and I would wander around messing with some of the free weights. I've always hated treadmills and stationary bikes. They make me feel like a hamster.

Have you ever seen one of those gym fail videos filled with little clips of people doing stupid things with the machines at the gym? Well, that was me at the gym. I understood body weight exercises like pull-ups and push-ups, but I had no idea what I was doing with those machines.

We were a few weeks into this when Angela decided to check out the group exercise classes included in our membership.

"I have never heard of a yoga class before. Do you want to do a yoga class with me?" she asked.

Let me be clear here. Angela knew yoga. She had done it for years when she was a teenager, but she was self-taught from books. She had never been to a class. I, on the other hand, had no idea what it was. I figured it was like step aerobics or cardio kickboxing.

"Sure, baby, I'll try yoga class with you."

I had no idea how much that choice would direct the course of my life.

Chapter Thirteen

The Masters say that one comes to yoga because of a sense of lack, the feeling that there is something wrong with the self or the world in general. This friction is what motivates us to find a better way. I stumbled into yoga, not knowing what I was in for, and left with the feeling that there were things wrong with me; very wrong. That is why I went back.

I remember standing there in class with my arms up, struggling and sweating profusely. I was thinking, "What's wrong with you? It's not like you're holding a dumbbell up there. It's just your own arms, and you can't hold them up. This is not good, man. Something is wrong here. You should be able to hold your own arms up."

The brain is so funny the way it works. Somehow, that thought led me to thinking, "If something was chasing you Jordan, intending to do you harm, and you needed to pull yourself over a wall or a fence to get away, I don't think you could do it." That one thought, more than any other, is why I went back. I was afraid that whatever was chasing me, literally or metaphorically, was going to catch up with me and get me.

When Angela and I moved to New Orleans, I left on good terms with Matthew. I tried calling him once while we were down there, but he was very short and cold toward me. He was not interested in talking to me. I was confused. I didn't know why, but it was obvious that he was upset with me about something. We had not talked since, and I missed him. I thought of him often but never worked up the nerve to connect with him.

Finally, after several years of isolation, I reached out. I found a card with two young boys laughing on it and sent it to him for his birthday. My message was simple, "Happy birthday. I'm not sure what happened and why we don't talk anymore, but I miss you, and whatever I did, I'm sorry." I signed it with my phone number and dropped it in the mail. I didn't think it would come to anything, but I had to make an attempt at regaining his friendship.

He did call and suggested we have a talk. I agreed and drove into the city to meet up with him for a beer and a chat. I arrived first. I'm always early, even when I try to be late. Matthew arrived shortly after with his new girlfriend. He was looking good, happy in a way I had never seen before. He was in love. I know that look. We had a little courteous chit chat about what we'd been up to before the real conversation started, and then I found out why we hadn't talked in so long.

In my last days at the pizza place, before I left to go work at the bank, Matthew and his long-term girlfriend were having troubles. She was a good friend to me too, and she talked with me one night about it. I told her, foolishly in hindsight, "Don't worry about it. I'll talk to him." I remember telling him, "Sometimes you just need to buy a girl some flowers or do something to show you love them and you are thinking about them." He didn't get it, and when he became frustrated with me, I let him change the topic and I let it go. I should have said more, but I didn't.

When they broke up while we were in New Orleans, it came up that I told her I would talk to him. I unintentionally had made their lack of communication worse because she thought I had explained her feelings to him, which I hadn't. For a long time, he held me partly responsible for their breakup.

All that was water under the bridge now though, and his heart was healed. He had a new love, and he had missed my friendship too, and that was it. We were fast friends again. I came to find out that he had started doing yoga too, which was strange. He was doing hot power yoga at a place in Cambridge, where they heated the room to one hundred degrees. I thought he was crazy. I thought "I sweat bullets in an air-conditioned room at the gym with the fans going, why on earth would I want to do it in a hundred degrees?" That sounded like torture, but he kept nagging me to come try class with him.

I'd given up on my sabbatical and reached out and connected with another human being. It felt good to have a friend again. Going to yoga at the gym was good for me, too. I felt like I was emerging from my chrysalis, wanting to feel connected to everything. So, I sought out my old method for connection again.

That year on my birthday, I got some ecstasy for Angela, Matthew, and a few other friends, and at some point that night, I agreed to try hot yoga. The next day, there was a class at four p.m. with one of Matthew's favorite teachers. When the sun came up and my friends went home, I got a few hours of sleep, showered, ate a little something, and then Angela and I drove into the city.

I didn't think doing hot yoga for the first time after rolling all night was a good idea, but I'd said I would do it, so I went. I remember checking into class, paying our fee, and standing awkwardly in line with my mat and blocks, waiting to get in.

Finally, the door to the studio opened and the previous class began pouring out; all these soaking wet people with their pupils dilated, looking like they were tripping with giant smiles on their pink faces. I had seen faces like that before at raves. "These people look high," I thought. "What are they doing in there?" I would soon find out.

We entered the room and found spaces, set up our mats, and sat down. When the teacher came in, Matthew waved her over and introduced her to Angela and me. She was a tall, lean, beautiful woman, and her eyes were otherworldly. She had a way of making an intense human connection in a matter of seconds, as if she was seeing right into your soul and ignoring your physical form.

She asked if we had done yoga before, as this was an intermediate class. I told her we had been taking classes a couple of times a week for a few months. I assured her I would try my best. She gave me a slight bow of her head and walked away.

It was so hot. I was sweating before we even started moving. The teacher said, "Come into downward facing dog! Right leg up! Left leg up! Step to the front of the mat! Stand up, bow, flat back, high plank, low plank, up dog, down dog, breathe in, breathe out!" she commanded. We repeated this sequence of postures until we were sweating, panting, and sighing with relief every time we landed back in down dog. "Warrior one, arms up, hold. Warrior two, arms wide," she said.

My arms were shaking, and my shoulders were screaming for me to stop. But I couldn't stop. I wouldn't stop. I was clenching and grinding my teeth, tensing my forehead, my eyes were sharp. And the sweat. The sweat is raining off! I felt like I was standing in the shower.

On some deep level, I was showering my insides, cleansing everything. We flowed through *surya namaskar B* (sun salutation B) over and over again at a steady, relentless pace.

My mind was filled with images I had seen on the Discovery Channel of Hindus, doing prostrations around holy sites. Then, we were twisting and turning and holding postures for what seemed like an eternity. We came to standing at the top of our mats, my head was swimming, everything looked foggy. "Is the room actually steamy, or are my eyes just shot from all the sweat in them?" I wondered.

I couldn't tell, but everything and everyone had an aura of golden light about them. Everything looked sparkly, radiant, and divine. My heart slammed in my chest. I did my best to stand on one foot like everyone else, but I was having enough trouble standing on two legs. So I just stood there like a soldier, breathing and feeling amazing. "Come to a high pushup, lower all the way to the ground," said the teacher. "Turn your head to one side."

"How strange," I thought. "Here I am, lying on a hard floor, face down in a pool of my own sweat, and I've never felt this good, ever." I felt plugged in and connected in a way that no drug had ever made me feel. But I couldn't have just walked in, laid down, and felt that good. I had to work to get to it. I did the work, and the feeling of connection was the reward.

We did a couple more poses, and then the teacher commanded us to roll over onto our backs. This was when I stopped participating in class. I rolled over onto my back and into pure bliss. Everyone in that crowded room faded away, the teacher's voice faded away. I lay there, staring up at the billowing clouds of fabric that draped the ceiling, running my fingers up and down my sweaty body, sending ripples of tingles through my body. After class, Matthew, Angela and myself went out for pho noodle soup. We sat and reveled in our experience, or at least Matthew and I did. Angela said, "That was the most masculine yoga ever!"

I became obsessed. I dropped my membership at the gym and started driving an hour into the city several times a week. The gym yoga classes just weren't good enough anymore. I had thought they were good until I experienced something better.

My old joke is that yoga is a lot like sex and pizza in that, even when it's bad, it's still pretty good. Angela always replies, "Apparently, you have never had bad sex." That is true.

Class on Sunday at four p.m. and pho noodles afterwards became a weekly ritual for the three of us. I would never have said this at the time, but it was like church for us. Those conversations we had over giant bowls of soup were priceless. I felt so inspired and alive. After years of feeling lost and confused, I'd found a new path, a new method to achieve what I'd always been seeking. The Truth.

Over the next few years, I would take many classes

with many teachers who all taught me lots of things, the majority of which were physical in nature, but they were always hinting at so much more under the surface. But that was it. Hints. They never gave me any more than that.

Over time, I became disappointed with my teachers, because I would ask them questions that they couldn't answer. I wasn't disappointed that they didn't know the answers. It's fine not to know. But instead of saying, "I don't know," they would make up answers. It's pretty obvious when someone doesn't know the answer and is bullshitting you. Still, though, I am grateful for these teachers, because they inspired me to search for my own answers. Fortunately for me, I am a Yogi in the digital age.

For most of history, those who wanted to study yoga devoted themselves to one guru or teacher, one lineage, one tradition. But with the advent of the internet, access to information has greatly expanded. I often joke about being a disciple of Swami Google. What a wonderful time to be a yoga student.

Now, we can learn from all of the texts, all the lineages, all the masters. It also means that there is lots of misinformation floating around out there, and it can be very confusing to try and make sense out of the thousands of years of history, tradition, knowledge, and practice that fall under the title of yoga.

Imagine a circle of people seated around a statue of an elephant. If I then ask those people to describe what they see, the people facing the elephant might say, "It has a big trunk and big ears". The people sitting behind it might agree that it has big ears, but they can't see the trunk, but they see its tail. The people in the front would say they don't see the tail.

Now, let's say that this elephant represents yoga, and the people seated around it are the masters. As a student, the more people you listen to, describing their point of view, the better your overall understanding will be. If you only listen to the people in the front, you will never know about the tail, and if you only listen to the people in the back, you will never learn about the trunk. The more perspectives you can listen to, the better your understanding will be.

So, what does the word "yoga" mean? Yoga is a sanskrit word that means union. The root word, "yo," means to join or to yoke; to connect an ox with a plow or a cart. Sanskrit is a Proto-Indo-European language, which means the English we speak today evolved from Sanskrit. When the yogic texts were written, humans lived in an agricultural society. Many of the ascetic yogis of the time were sustenance farmers, meaning they grew their own food to survive, not for sale or profit. Many of the metaphors relate to this lifestyle.

In order to understand what you are yoking or joining or bringing into union, you must first understand a little of the common philosophical views of the time. The oldest religious texts are called the *Vedas*, which, for the most part, talk about God, how to worship, and what to expect from the afterlife. *Veda* translates to knowledge, and there are four *Vedas*.

Look, I'm no scholar, but I will give you my best shot at this. *The Rigveda, the Yajurveda, the Samaveda, and the Atharvaveda.*

The *Rigveda* is the oldest religious text in the world that is still used today. It is largely about divine hymns.

The *Yajurveda* details how one should worship the divine.

The *Samaveda* is the basis of Indian classical music, laying out the various melodies and chanting structures.

The *Atharvaveda* is the last and most recent. This text focuses on the general duties of the court priests, including how to perform weddings, funerals, royal rituals, and initiations.

Each of the four Vedas is broken up into four subdivisions: *Samhita-Mantra, Aranyakas, Brahmanas,* and *Upanishads.*

Sanhita-Mantra is the chanting of various names for the divine.

Aranyakas is the portion of the texts concerned with how to perform ritual ceremonies and sacrifices.

Brahmanas is the section detailing how the Brahman (priests) should perform the ceremonies and for what purpose.

And the last section, the *Upanishads* (at the foot of the master), discusses the philosophy and spiritual knowledge of meditation.

The *Vedas* are said to be *śruti*. *Śruti* means that these texts were heard from the divine. The Rishis, or "great sages," would go into the forest and meditate. While in deep meditation, these verses were "heard." In a largely oral tradition, they were handed down from teacher to student for the last three thousand years, give or take five hundred years.

When young Brahman enter the period of *Brahmacharya* (on the path to Brahman) at age eight, they learn to recite the *Vedas* verbatim. They chant, and chant, and chant for twelve years without knowing what any of these mantras actually mean.

At the end of this period, at age twenty, they are given a choice. They can continue their studies to become a Brahman and learn what it is they have been chanting, or they can become a householder, and live a normal life with a family and a career. If you're reading this and wondering, "How did we get from the *Vedas* to sweaty bodies moving and breathing in a hot room?", I did too. It's a long story. About three thousand years of human history. I have pursued little else for the last fifteen years.

After that first hot yoga class, yoga took over my life. Not all at once, it was gradual, but once I was hooked, that was it. There was no going back. One famous yoga adage is that "we must unlearn our learning," but you can't unlearn the things yoga shows you. It's not just knowledge. It's not theoretical. It's actual. Once the Truth acts on you, it is very hard to see things any other way.

It's like that scene in The Matrix when Morpheus asks Neo if he wants the blue pill or the red pill. If Neo takes the blue pill, then he goes back to sleep and believes whatever he wants to believe. If Neo chooses the red pill, there's no going back, and he gets to see how deep the Truth is.

I'll say to my students, "You think you come here to exercise, but you have no idea what you're getting yourself into. You just wanted a flat belly and a tight butt, but you are going to wake up and realize you are God." They laugh. And then I say, "I'm not joking, but you don't have to believe me, keep it up and you'll see."

And that is the power of putting philosophy into

practice. Knowing knowledge is good and important, but without practice, there is no experience, and experience is what makes the knowledge real and tangible. Without the experience, the knowledge just seems theoretical.

Yoga says, "Don't believe, try, and see what happens." What happens is it proves itself. Belief has nothing to do with it. It just is. So when you take knowledge and add experience, you get wisdom. It doesn't matter what anyone else thinks about it. You've been through it. You have lived it. You have aligned your reality to the Truth.

Chapter Fourteen

The *Vedas* were compiled from 1500 BCE to about 800 BCE. About six hundred years after the *Veda* texts came the *Vedānta* texts. *Vedānta* means "the end of the *Vedas*". At this point, the sages and scholars had focused their efforts towards understanding God and death for about two thousand years. They felt like they had a pretty good understanding of all of that, and so decided to turn their efforts towards understanding the material world. The *Sāṅkhya* school of metaphysics was next.

Sāṅkhya means "knowledge of self through right discrimination." Perhaps what I love most about this text is the incredibly logical way they arrive at conclusions. Furthermore, they go to great lengths to explain the proper way to gain "right knowledge."

In the very first verse, they lay out the reason for inquiry into understanding the manifest world: "From the torment caused by the three kinds of pain, proceeds a desire for inquiry into the means of terminating them. The subject matter of this study would not be inquired into if there existed no pain in this world, or, if existent, its removal were not desired, or, if desired, it's removal were impossible. It cannot be said that there is no pain, or that its removal is not desired (as these are opposed to experienced facts)." -

verse 1

In verse 4, they explain the means by which they came to these understandings. "Perception, inference, and valid testimony are the means; (by these) all other means of right cognition too are established (as they are included in the above three); proof is intended to be of three kinds. It is through the proofs that the provables are established."

When I found this text, I wanted to jump up and yell, "Yes!" These people were speaking a language that made sense to me. I had found a doctrine, not based on faith and belief, but one like science, based on proof and consensus. Proof that comes from what we experience with our eyes and ears, what we can infer from our sensory experiences, and valid testimony from other's experiences.

And so, with this clear intention stated and the procedure agreed upon, they set out to create a map of the Universe from the most subtle to the most gross, and they came up with the twenty-five *Tattvas*. *Tattvas* translates as "Thatnesses."

1. *Puruṣa* – Spirit. Consciousness. As I said before, consciousness is the void. An infinite, homogenous nothingness, a unified field of energy. Consciousness has no cause. It always has been. Everything that is, comes from this void.

2. *Prakṛti* – The seed of all matter.

Earlier, I referred to *puruṣa* as *shiva* and *prakṛti* as *shakti*. That is because later, when the Tantrikas take the twenty-five *tattvas* to the next level and expand on the understanding in the thirty-six *tattvas*, they refer to *puruṣa* and *prakṛti* in these terms. If you're confused, don't worry, keep reading.

All of *prakṛti* is controlled by three forces known as *guṇa* (quality or attribute). That is to say the entire material world from planets and stars to trees and humans are all controlled by the three *guṇa*. *Puruṣa* is entirely separate and unaffected by the *guṇa*.

It is for this reason that yoga philosophy, at this point in history, is a dualistic philosophy. There is spirit and there is matter, and the two have nothing to do with each other. When the three *guṇa* are in balance, nothing exists. It is the fluctuation in balance between the *guṇa* that allows for things to come into being. The three *guṇa* are *tamas*, *rajas*, and *sattva*.

Tamas is sluggish and obscuring. It is related to inertia in that, unless affected by one of the other two, *tamas* will persist.

Rajas is activity. *Rajas* is exciting and mobile.

Sattva is purity, tranquility, and lucidity.

As I said, when these forces are in balance and homogenous, there are no things, just a unified field of energy. All things go through these forces, and that is the cause of change.

So, when the star that I spoke of in the introduction is in the nebulous stage, it is *tamas*. When gravity begins to work on the dust and the hydrogen, it is *rajas*. When fusion and gravity come into balance, it is *sattva*. As they go out of balance at the supernova stage, it is back to *rajas*. And then at the black hole, it is back to *tamas*.

Sāṇkhya then maps a human being from subtle to gross.

3. Intellect (*Buddhi*) – one step more dense than *puruṣa* (consciousness).

4. Ego Identity (*Ahankāra* – the " I" maker)

5. Mind (*Manas*)

Instruments of knowing:

6. Ears (*Śrotra*)

7. Nose (*Ghrāṇa*)

8. Tongue (*Rasanā*)

9. Eyes (*Cakṣus*)

10. Skin (*Tvak*)

Instruments of action:

11. Voice, speech (*Vāk*)

12. Hands, manipulation (*Pāni*)

13. Feet, locomotion (*Pāda*)

14. Genitals, reproduction (*Upastha*)

15. Anus, elimination (*Pāyu*)

The Ego through the senses experiences the five subtle elements:

16. Sound (*Śabda*)

17. Smell (*Gandha*)

18. Taste (*Rasa*)

19. Form (*Rūpa*)

20. Touch (*Sparśa*)

The Intellect understands the subtle elements:

21. Space (*Ākāśa*)

22. Air (*Vāyu*)

23. Fire (*Agni*)
24. Water (*Āpaḥ*)
25. Earth (*Pṛthvī*)

Then, in the *sāṇkhya* view, there are layers of the human being called *kośa*. The five *kośa* are:

1. *Annamaya kośa* – the physical body; the food sheath. The most dense and so associated with the Earth element.

2. *Pranamaya kośa* – the energy body; the vital sheath. It is more subtle, and it flows, and therefore, it is associated with the Water element.

3. *Manomaya kośa* – the mind and senses; the mental sheath. Even more subtle and associated with the Fire element.

4. *Vijñānamaya kośa* – Intelligence; the intuitive sheath. More subtle and associated with the Air element.

5. *Anandamaya kośa* – Consciousness; the bliss sheath. The most subtle, and therefore associated with the Ether or Space element.

Note that in each word, part of the word is *"maya"*. *Maya* means nature, but it also means illusion, because nature is an illusion laid on top of Truth. All of these layers are illusions that hide our true nature. Remove the illusion, and you are left with the Truth.

One might identify with the body, mind, thoughts and emotions, but this is an illusion. What we all are behind these illusions is *puruṣa* (soul, spirit, consciousness, awareness). Identifying as anything other than this puts us out of alignment with the Truth. When we are out of alignment with what is, this causes friction. And that friction is the source of our suffering.

The spirit is a solitary neutral spectator. It does not act, only observes. For this reason, it is often referred to as the witness. The part of us that is always in the background, watching, unaffected by the play of the *guṇa* (what is happening).

In the *sāṇkhya* view, the best course of action to eliminate suffering is to follow the path of renunciation. That is to say, deny the body, mind, and senses, because they are all traps that lead to delusion. Deny the world and social obligations, because these too are illusions.

I would like to say at this point that while this is an effective way to achieve liberation, it is not the only way, nor do I think it is the best way. The path to renunciation causes one not to live; to renounce life, wait for death, and hope for a more fortunate birth next time around. Remember, they were ascetics; monks with no family, no job, and no possessions, a total renunciation of life.

This brings us to the *Yoga Sūtra* of Patañjali. *Sāṇkhya* is the philosophy, the *Yoga Sūtra* are how we put that philosophy into practice. It is a method for living the philosophy. What is a *sūtra*? *Sūtra* means thread. It is where we get the modern word "suture". A *sūtra* is an aphorism. A short phrase that a teacher can say to a student to remind them of a larger teaching.

The first time one reads the *Yoga Sūtra*, one would find it very hard to understand. Maybe you have read them and had this experience. That's quite by design. They are cryptic on purpose. You can feel the truth of the words but have trouble grasping the meaning. This was to keep anyone who was able to read them from understanding. It was a way of keeping the knowledge from the uninitiated. They were meant to be explained to a student by a teacher, not to be read and understood as common knowledge by anyone.

It wasn't until I had read the *Yoga Sūtra* many times that it occurred to me that it is actually written in this way. It is written as a conversation between a teacher and a student, but only the teacher's answers are written. In between each verse, there is an implied question. As a reader, I would encourage you to not read it as a manual, but as a dialogue, and in between each verse, contemplate what is the next logical question. Ask that question before you read the next verse. It has been my experience that the next verse answers that question.

Imagine a teacher and student sitting cross-legged, facing one another in a temple or outdoors in nature. The teacher begins with verse 1: *"Atha yoga anushasanam"* or "With great respect and love, now the blessings of yoga instruction are offered."

What would be the logical question the student would ask after that statement? "What is yoga?" Isn't it?

Verse 2 states: *"Yogas citta vrtti nirodhah"* or "Yoga is the calming of the fluctuations of the mind," answering the implied question.

What would you ask next? Is it "Then what happens?"

Verse 3 states: *"Tada drashtuh svarupe avasthanam"* or "The seer is revealed, resting in its own essential nature, and one realizes the True self."

And then the student asks, "What is the True self?"

Verse 4 states: *"Vritti sarupyam itaratra"* or "At all other times, the Self appears to assume the form of thought vacillations and the True self is lost."

See what I mean?

When you read the *Yoga Sūtra*, and please read them, try to come up with a question before you read the next verse. If the next verse doesn't answer your question, it will help you figure out what the right question is. You may ask the wrong question. This happens often in the process of learning.

The *Yoga Sūtra* has four parts, or *pāda*. *Pāda* means foot, but in this case, it means part or chapter.

The first is the *Samādhi Pāda*. After explaining what yoga is and how it works and what it does, Patañjali goes on to say that the best thing one can do to accomplish yoga is *samādhi*.

What is *samādhi*? If you look it up, you will probably find one-word translations, such as bliss or oneness. And while these words are not inaccurate, I feel they are incomplete. The problem is that no words can convey the actual experience. Words are symbols, and we have to agree on those symbols to have an understanding.

In addition, *samādhi* is a non-verbal state, so anyone who experiences it has a hard time finding words to describe it. To enter into a state of *samādhi*, one is going back through the *kośa* (sheaths), from gross to subtle.

If you remember from the twenty-five *tattva*, language is something that occurs in the mind. When we are in *samādhi*, we are at the most subtle level, consciousness, *puruṣa*. There is no mental function, no sense of "I," no intellect, just awareness. In order to express the experience with words, one must condense it through intellect, and then through the duality that comes through a sense of "me," and then into the mind, as words. In that process, much is lost.

Think of a high-resolution photo that you send by SMS. It's crystal clear on your end, but on the recipient's end, it's kind of grainy. They can see it, but much is lost in the transmission. There is also an old stigma around the discussion of *samādhi*, and many people are reluctant to say they have experienced it; that somehow saying it out loud makes them arrogant.

This is absurd. Everyone has experienced *samādhi* at some point in their life. They may not use that term to describe it, but every human, whether or not they practice yoga, experiences it at some point.

As one of my teachers likes to point out, "Every human does yoga, but some of us practice it consciously." Yoga practice is about practicing very human things to get better at them, including *samādhi*.

Patañjali lays out ten stages of *samādhi*. They are of two types. Stages one through eight are *sabīja* (with seed), and nine and ten are *nirbīja* (without seed). The seed is the ego. The difference is the sense of "I." Is the ego still in play or not?

The order of *tattvas* from subtle to gross goes, *puruṣa* (consciousness) to *prakṛti* (all matter) to *buddhi* (intellect) to *ahamkara* (ego) to *manas* (mind). *Samādhi* is when one works their way back from mind through ego, through intellect and into *puruṣa* (consciousness).

Have you ever been taking a nap on a warm afternoon, maybe in a hammock, outside or on the couch with the doors and the windows open? You are completely relaxed and at ease, and you are drifting in and out of sleep. When you are conscious, you are aware of the environment.

Maybe you hear a lawn mower in the distance, or maybe you can hear children playing. You hear the wind in the trees or smell flowers or fresh cut grass on the breeze. You are blissfully aware of your senses, but you are not thinking about them with words. You are simply perceiving the present moment.

If you've had an experience like this, then you've experienced *Samprajnata Samādhi*, the first of the ten stages of *samādhi*). The early stages of *samādhi* are like this. One is aware of their senses and of the Self, but there is an absence of thought. I think everyone falls into this state at some point in life without trying.

Asamprajnata is a little bit harder to stumble upon, but if you have practiced yoga, or more specifically, *yoga nidra*, you may have experienced it without having the language to describe it.

Often, a student will come up to me after class with a look of confusion on their face and ask, "What was that? Did I fall asleep? Where did I go?"

And then I ask, "Did you fall asleep? You know the experience of sleep. You do it all the time. Was it sleep?"

"No," they reply.

And then I explain. "'Where did I go?' is the right question. You transcended your ego and lost your sense of self, and yet were still intellectually aware of the experience. The natural world faded away with your senses, and you lost all sense of space and time. Then the sound of my voice telling you to take a deep breath brought you back from there, through the *ahamkara* (the "I" maker) and into mind, and from there, back to your physical body and senses. All that happened in a flash, and it left you feeling a little startled?" They nod slowly. I tell them it is good progress.

How about you, dear reader? Have you had a similar experience? I try to spend a little time in this state every day. I do it to remind myself of the oneness of all things. When that is fresh in my memory, I don't act as an individual, but as a whole. I am not this body, mind, or intellect. These things will die. I will die, but that is not me. We are *puruṣa*. Inside each of us is a *jīvā* (soul). You know this is true. You can deny that you feel it if you want, but I will call bullshit. You might not want to admit it for whatever reasons, but I know you can feel it. *Samādhi* connects our *jīvā* with *atmān*, the collective human consciousness. In the *nirbija* (without seed) stages of *samādhi* (stages nine and ten), *atmān* merges into *brāhman* (the universal consciousness).

I've only experienced this once, and I will be honest here. I ate psilocybin mushrooms and meditated for the entire trip. The experience was so profound that when I came back to the physical, I promised I would teach about it in every class I taught for the week, which was about twenty classes at that time. Every time, words fell short.

We always come back. We cannot stay in the state of *samādhi*. It's transitory, just like everything else. However, when we come back, the experience makes it very difficult to be selfish. It just seems so small and petty, because it is. Ultimately, removing the illusion of duality and ending our selfishness is liberation from suffering.

It's very difficult to get to a point where one can experience *samādhi* and understand the experience. I had been practicing for years before it happened. Patañjali acknowledges this, and in the second *pāda*, he lays out two paths to this end: *kriyā* and *ashtānga*.

Kriyā yoga consists of three practices. *Svādhyāya* (self-study), *tapas* (austerity), and *Īśvara praṇidhāna* (dedication to the divine ideal).

Svādhyāya: to study oneself. Watch yourself very closely, every moment of every day. Watch your thoughts. Watch your emotions that arise from your thoughts. Watch your conditioned reactions to external stimulations and situations. Watch your actions. Question everything you take for granted about yourself.

As you do this, you will begin to build up a space between the thinker and the thought, and because space is time, you will begin to move slower through life. We must move slower to maintain this witness consciousness. In this way, we can begin to see things about our personalities that we have been hiding from ourselves and denying, and also gain clarity about what makes us tick.

Svādhyāya also means to study texts yourself. Don't just listen to what your teachers have to say in commentary. Read and study yourself to gain your own understanding and insight.

I often do a meditation practice that brings to light, out of the subconscious and into thought, the things I am hiding from myself or things I am in denial about.

It goes like this. As with most meditation practices, sit comfortably either cross-legged on a cushion or in a chair with the feet flat on the floor. Rest your hands in a comfortable position and close your eyes. Turn your awareness inwards and become aware of your breathing, just your natural breath. Take a few moments to slow down and let your awareness become focused.

Then, begin to repeat the phrase, "I will see myself

clearly," internally. How many times can you repeat it before you have another thought? Sooner or later, you will stop repeating the phrase and begin thinking about other things, and, sooner or later, you will realize that you are no longer repeating the phrase.

This is the important moment. Work your way back. What were you thinking about when you first stopped repeating the phrase? Not always, but often enough, that first thought is something you need to examine more closely. Something in that first thought is distorted and needs to be brought into the light. It can now be seen clearly.

I was teaching this technique in a workshop once and a student said, "So I am going to wind up knowing a bunch of stuff that I don't like about myself? Great." This surprised me. I responded. "Would you rather this continue to influence you unconsciously, causing you and those around you suffering? If you can see it, you can be done with it."

Once you see it clearly, it's done. It's over. Sure, you may feel embarrassed or disappointed momentarily, but those feelings are the very ones that will ensure you will change.

If you want to be serious about your yoga practice, read. I can't stress this enough. Read everything you can get your eyes on. Struggle and strive to grasp the concepts. Work hard to fit these pieces together into comprehension. Be emphatic in your quest for truth, have a burning desire to achieve liberation from suffering. This is *tapas*, the second practice.

The root word, "*tap*," means to burn. The underlying

meaning is that you would walk through fire or over hot coals to gain an insight. You are willing to try any austerity in the pursuit of your understanding, able to endure and overcome any hardship, like giving up coffee for forty days.

Forty days is a typical length of time for a *sādhanā* (practice). *Tapas* will shake you out of your routine, out of your habits, out of complacency, because it is only in adversity that our mettle is tested. We take up austerity to aid in our *svādhyāya* (self-study).

You can think of it in one of two ways. First, you can commit to giving up something for forty days, such as alcohol or meat. You see how that affects you. At the end of the *sādhanā*, maybe you have a drink or maybe you don't, but you use this period of reflection to get clarity around the issue and make a conscious choice about where you will be going forward.

Alternatively, you can take up a new behavior for forty days. You could chant a mantra one hundred and eight times a day, or practice *asāna* (postures) for forty days in a row. You observe, learn, and grow through commitment. We all crave the security of a routine, but when things are too routine for too long, we may become bored and apathetic (*tamas*). Taking up a form of *tapas* (austerity) can help change that perspective.

A student once asked me, "What if your whole life feels like *tapas*?" Great question. We all go through periods where we feel like the Universe is just dumping problem after problem on us, even though that is not the Truth. If you're feeling a bit beat up by life, then you have enough fodder for self-study (*svādhyāya*) already. No need to heap more on top of it, unless this has been going on for a long time. In that case, it can be empowering to choose austerity. Stuff might be happening to you, but at least with this one thing, you are choosing to do it.

The third practice is *Īśvara praṇidhāna*. It means "Surrender to the Lord." Place oneself under the fullness of the divine. Oh, how I have struggled with this. Remember, I was raised in a religious household, and I vehemently rejected the notion of God and anything that smelled like religion. Because of this, I ignored this advice from the great master Patañjali for many years. I avoided the whole concept. And for now, I'm going to avoid it again. I am putting it on the back burner to simmer. I will come back to it later in the story.

Chapter Fifteen

I continued practicing yoga in the city a couple of days a week. Eventually, the driving and traffic became too much. So I found a hot yoga studio closer to where I lived. I was going there a few nights a week after work, and still going into the city on Sundays. I started working the front desk at the nearby studio in exchange for class.

This went on for a few years while I continued to slave away at the trombone factory, until finally, I was promoted out of the buffing room. They moved me around to various jobs, and I mastered every one of them. This earned me the title of Assistant Production Manager.

Angela and I bought a house. It was the cutest little A-frame house. I loved that house. It was essentially a one-bedroom with a loft, and a balcony overlooking the backyard. It had a finished basement. I had done it. I had chosen to choose life, and I had done everything society had told me would make me happy. I was married. I had a good job. I had bought a home, and I was only twenty-eight years old. I was feeling pretty good for a while, but after a year of playing house, I started to become restless. My twenty-ninth birthday was approaching, and it seemed I was having my midlife crisis a bit early.

You see, twenty-seven is the age that several rock stars

were when they died. Jim Morrison, Jimi Hendrix, Kurt Cobain, and more all died at the age of twenty-seven. For a long time, I was operating under the assumption that I would be famous and dead before I was thirty. Instead, I was doing hard work and home improvements and grinding it out at work six days a week to pay for it all.

I started thinking, "Is this it? Am I just supposed to do this for the next thirty-five years until I can retire, bitter and used up like the guys I was working with?" I was standing on the front porch thinking this when I looked up at the sky and said out loud, "There has got to be more to my life than this!"

A few weeks later, I had tickets to see Radiohead in concert. Angela can't stand Radiohead, so I asked Matthew to go with me. After the show, we were hanging out at my house, chatting. Matthew had started teaching yoga at this point. I was feeling restless and unfulfilled currently, and I became reminiscent about all the fun times we'd had in the past, working together. I told him that if there ever was an opportunity for us to work together again, I would like that.

"You want to teach yoga?" he asked.

I said, "No, I do not want to teach yoga," laughing.

"Why not?" he questioned.

"Dude, you know me. I've got a big mouth that often gets me into trouble. I don't think that putting myself in front of a group of people would turn out well."

Matthew, ever the salesman, was just like my father. They both had a way of trapping me with their sound logic in a way that I could not refute.

He said, "Why don't you let me teach you? And if you don't like it or don't want to do it, you don't have to." How could I argue with that?

Matthew gathered a small group of aspiring teachers together to train. All of them had completed two hundred hours of teacher training, except for me. After just a few weekends of training, I was given my first opportunity to substitute teach a class. I was so nervous. I felt totally unqualified and completely unprepared, but Matthew assured me, he would be right there in the back, and if I got lost or confused, to just look at him, and he would help me out.

So, with one friendly face in the room, I stepped up to the front and in a loud, clear, and confident voice said, "Hello, my name is Jordan. Let's come into down dog and get started." I remember skipping something in the sequence at one point and looking to Matthew with a "what do I do now" expression. He helped me reorder things quickly, and the class went on.

"Just be yourself," Matthew had told me. But being myself has always gotten me into trouble. "Teach from what you know," he had told me. But what do I know? I know that my favorite part of a class is when the teacher tells an insightful story. I hadn't learned how to do this yet. All I had learned was how to call the poses, and I wasn't very good at that.

"What do I know? What do I know?" I asked myself. "These people don't know anything about you, so tell them something," I thought. I put them into half pigeon and said, "None of you know me very well. I'm a metal worker. I make trumpets and trombones.

"It's a funny thing, working with metal. When you shape metal, you bend it, you twist it, and hammer it into a shape. The more you work it, the more the molecules become compressed. It becomes hard and then brittle. And if you keep working it, it will eventually crack and break, and all the work you put in up to that point is wasted.

"But if you stop before it gets brittle and breaks, and you heat it up until it glows cherry red, the molecules spread out, and the metal softens and relaxes into a new shape. You can continue to shape it and do this indefinitely until you end with the shape you intended all along.

"I was thinking about this while I was working the other day, and I thought, you know, we are not so different from this metal. Life twists us and bends us and hammers us, and our molecules become compressed. We become hard and brittle, and eventually, we break. But if we come in here in this heat until our cheeks glow red, then our molecules spread out and can relax and soften. And we can go on being shaped by life without breaking under the stress of it."

All the room was silent except for the hum of the heater. I swallowed. I didn't know if they had heard me or not, or if I was speaking sense or nonsense, but I finished the class, and thanked them with a bow. The room erupted into applause, much to my surprise.

I was offered a slot teaching at six a.m., an hour drive from home. I was used to being at the shop by five a.m., so that worked fine for me. I could teach a yoga class and be at work at the shop by eight with everyone else. The first time I taught at six, I had three students, and the second time, I had only one show up for class. The studio's policy was that three people needed to be in attendance for class to happen.

Looking back now, the decision I made at that moment was an important one. It was six a.m. The student had shown up to learn. I was there with nowhere else to be. Was I there to help people or to make money? Definitely the former. So I said to the student, "I'm here and you're here. Do you want to do this?"

They said, "Yes."

And so we did. We had a wonderful practice together.

More and more students were showing up for class, and soon, I was teaching classes of forty to fifty people. I began teaching three six a.m. classes a week,

Then Saturdays, then evenings too. It wasn't long before I was about fifty/fifty, teaching yoga and making trombones. I loved it, but I felt like a bit of a fraud. I hadn't ever completed a yoga teacher training. I had no credentials, and yet the students would look at me and could see something in me that I didn't believe in myself, like Angela had before. And like Angela, I didn't want to disappoint them.

So, I decided to work to earn that look. I was going to be the best yogi, the very best human being I could be. My best self. When two of my favorite teachers offered a two-hundred-hour training, I jumped at the opportunity.

I apparently had some natural teaching ability, but this first training gave me skills and knowledge to enhance that ability. It also gave me confidence. Most importantly, though, I had my first experience of *samādhi* (supra-consciousness) during this training.

It was at the end of a very long day. I had taught two classes early and then drove to training where we practiced teaching about a million sun salutations. Then we took an intermediate class in the afternoon, followed by the relax and renew class in the evening.

By the time I got to the last class, there was nothing relaxing or renewing about it for me. My body was spent, I was dehydrated and having muscle cramps all over, but was trying my very best to be a good little soldier. I was trying to participate in the class, but it must have been obvious that I was suffering.

In a sweet, simple act of kindness, understanding, and empathy, the teacher placed her hands on my back and quietly whispered to me in a motherly tone, "It's okay. You don't have to continue. You've done enough. Rest."

The teacher put on a piece of classical music in *savāsana* (corpse pose), and one moment I was listening to the music, and the next, I was gone. I was smeared across the cosmos. Then, in a flash, I was back. I tried to dismiss the experience as falling asleep, but it wasn't sleep.

It was also during this training that I read the *Yoga Sūtra* for the first time and began to live my life by the *aṣṭāṅga* (the eight-limb path). After Patañjali explains *kriyā yoga*, he lays out the eight-limb practice or the *aṣṭāṅga*.

I like to think I can picture him being like, "Okay, okay. So you've been trying the three practices of *kriyā yoga*, and you still are not experiencing *samādhi*. Now, do these eight things, and no matter how entangled you are in karma (cause and effect), you will get there."

The first of the eight limbs, or spokes of the wheel, as I like to think of them, is *yama*. *Yama* is the moral code of ethics for the yogi. The *yama* are all about how you treat others. For every action you put out into the world, you plant a seed for that action to flower in your own experience.

Ahiṃsā is the first of the five *yama*, and it means "do no harm." Do no harm with thought, words, or actions. This might seem like an obvious one. After all, we are raised in a society that punishes unsanctioned violence. We're not supposed to go around punching people in the face.

Even though I was raised Christian, which also preaches of peace, I was very violent. My unchecked anger was always simmering just under the surface, and it didn't take much to set me off. I would boil over in a snap. So much so that Angela and Matthew called me "The Rage" as a derogatory nickname when my temper would flare up. It was even taking a toll on my physical health. By twenty-five, I already had hypertension bad enough for medication.

I was always ready for a fight, because I'd put myself in opposition to the world. I was fighting myself. The ability to respond to violence with kindness is what it means to be human. I wasn't being human. I was being like an animal, responding to violence with violence. The flood of endorphins made me feel powerful and strong for a moment, but when it wore off, I was left feeling terrible, sick, and disappointed.

I had accepted that this was just another part of living in this shitty existence, and that I was standing up for myself. I had it so backwards. I was causing the suffering. I was raging against it. It wasn't the world. The world has no problems. Human beings have inner conflicts that we project onto the world. I learned this through the experience of practicing *ahiṃsā*.

I began my practice by focusing on my interactions with my coworkers. Up to this point, we had all communicated through a slew of jokes, insults, backhanded comments, and insulting, degrading nicknames. I committed to stop participating in this, and to meet all my coworker's actions with kindness or indifference.

This was actually pretty easy. It felt good, like something inside me relaxed a little bit. I aided my efforts by taking up a meditation practice. In this practice, I would hold someone I loved or respected in my awareness until I began to feel the love and appreciation in my body. Then I would bring my awareness to someone I fought with regularly at work and would hold the feeling of love in my body while I thought of them.

Through this process, I began to see this person as a child. I saw the boy within the man that, just like me, wanted to be happy, and was doing everything he could to avoid suffering. I can't tell you we became best friends after this, because we didn't, but I began to see that much of what irritated me about him were behaviors and actions that I too was guilty of.

Other people are simply mirrors. They reflect back to us what we want to be, and what we don't want to be. My animosity towards the man melted away, I found that I could easily occupy the same space and communicate with him without being in fight mode.

My behavior had changed so dramatically at work that people actually said to me, "What is up with you, man? You've changed." I was trying. It was not easy work. It took consistent effort over a period of time until it became my new way of being. It is so much easier to just do what you've always done.

I can't stand the saying, "People don't change." People

don't change because they don't want to do the work. It's not a lack of ability to change. It's laziness. Change is always happening. We can participate in it or not. We can continue the same old patterns over and over and accept the suffering that it causes to us and those around us, or we can do the work to liberate ourselves.

Everything changed when I realized that there was no one to blame but myself for my reality. All of my happiness and all of my suffering wasn't because of external circumstances. It was all my own doing. There is no savior, because no one can save you from yourself. All the pain and anger I'd been dealing with for so long was no one's fault but my own. The good news was the Truth that if I had gotten myself into this mess, I could get myself out of it. That was my inspiration, my motivation, and my liberation.

The second obvious behavior I addressed when I began to practice *ahiṃsā* was my road rage. It usually takes time and patience to change a behavior. It does not happen by simply deciding to change. The decision is just the first step, then you must work at it. Think of your behavior as a groove, carved into a path. It is much easier for the wheel to follow the old groove. If you want to change, then you must pull the wheel of your life out of that groove and carve a new one by driving over the new one again and again.

At first, when I would see someone driving poorly, my wheel would fall into the old groove, and I would do all the things I had always done. I would scream, yell, and give them the finger. Afterwards, after the emotion had passed, I would say to myself, "I thought you were not going to do that anymore." That went on for a while, always catching myself after.

Eventually, with patience and persistence, I was able to catch myself in the emotion. I would try to stop myself from acting out the emotion and, instead of swearing and yelling, I would grip the steering wheel tight and grumble. Then I began to try to influence the emotion. I would say, "Have a nice day", but my tone still said, "Fuck you."

Then I started to make other changes, like leaving earlier to get where I was going, so I wouldn't feel rushed. I stopped driving on the highway and took secondary roads instead. I listened to audiobooks and podcasts and tried to enjoy my time in the car.

Now, I'm the guy that pulls over to let the person tailgating me go. I have no road rage. It was a process. It's not about instant success. If we try to change overnight, we will become frustrated and be unproductively hard on ourselves. It takes time. Be patient but relentless.

The only time we actually fail is when we fail to try. As long as we continue to try, we will succeed. Paraphrasing Thomas Edison, "I didn't fail a thousand times. The light bulb was an invention with a thousand steps."

Chapter Sixteen

The second *yama* is *satya*, which means "truthfulness." Again, this might seem obvious, but look a little deeper. Yes, it is important to speak the truth and to not tell lies to others, but we must also align our reality to the Truth so that we are not deluding ourselves. If we are Truth, then speaking the Truth comes naturally.

Think of a time when you lied to manipulate the outcome of a situation. Perhaps you told yourself it was just a harmless little white lie. Maybe you decided to omit some information because you decided the person didn't really need to know the whole story. Sometimes, we tell ourselves that we are doing the other person a favor by not telling them something that might hurt their feelings. Other times, we tell a lie to get what we want.

We see cause and effect where there is none. We think, "I told a little lie, but I got what I wanted." The problem is that this goes against the way everything else in the Universe works. Like produces like, and the cause is visible in the effect it creates.

For example, you wouldn't plant an apple seed and be surprised if an apple tree grew where you planted the seed. It would be quite odd, however, if you planted an apple seed and it grew into a tomato plant. But that is essentially what

Jordan P. Lashley

I am talking about.

If you think you can tell a lie and have it produce something positive, you are not seeing clearly. A lie is always a negative. It can only produce a negative outcome. When we tell a lie, we are planting a seed that, when the conditions are right, will eventually flower and produce something negative in our existence.

It is sometimes difficult to see this happening because often, right after we plant a lie seed, some other positive seed from the past flowers and produces a positive result in our existence. The lie and the positive result had nothing to do with each other, but because they happened one right after the other, people often put them together as cause and effect. This flaw in perception distorts reality from the Truth. This then puts us in conflict with what is, which causes friction that we feel as suffering.

I lied all the time growing up. I felt like I had to in order to do the things I wanted to do. I lied so much that it became a compulsion. I would lie for no reason, and I lied to myself. My reality was so far from True that I would lie and then ask myself why so many negative things were happening in my life. I would ask why the Universe was out to get me. I was so blind that I couldn't see it was me. I was the maker of my own suffering. The Universe wasn't out to get me. I was sabotaging myself and drifting further and further from the Truth.

When something is running straight, another way to say that is that it is running true. If it is not straight or true, then it's got a little wobble in it. If that wobble is not corrected, it gets worse. With every revolution, it will get bigger and bigger, and more and more violent until something breaks. I've seen it happen many times at the trombone shop, I always had to correct the wobble and get it running true before I could do anything else. When something is not running true on a machine or in life, it is dangerous, and someone always ends up getting hurt.

Even when I lied or omitted the truth to save someone's feelings, it didn't seem to work. Here's the deal. If we can help a person get true and run straight and we don't, are we really doing them a favor? Aren't we just avoiding getting intimately personal with them out of our own fear and insecurity?

Think of it like this. Let's say you are out for a meal with a loved one and they get some food on their face. You would just tell them, "You have a little something there," and point to your own face, or if you were very close, you might even reach out and wipe it off for them.

Now let's suppose it's a business luncheon with coworkers and important clients and someone gets a little food on their cheek. Would you still tell them? Would you be worried about embarrassing them? Eventually, they're going to go to the restroom and see it, and they are going to feel embarrassed and hurt that no one told them. They will wonder if everyone was laughing at them. The point is that we wouldn't save them from anything by not telling them. In fact, we make it worse by letting it continue.

It is so much easier to see when someone else is not seeing clearly than it is to see it in ourselves. It is our duty to help each other out and to value when someone is honest with us. We must let them know when there is food on their face.

In the *Book of Joy*, Bishop Desmond Tutu talks a lot

about *ubuntu*. *Ubuntu* means "people are people through other people". We can't do it alone. We need each other to be our best selves. Trying to do life alone put me on a path filled with suffering. I was headed to an early death or jail, and the more I thought about myself, the more miserable I became. The more we care for each other on a human level, the happier we become.

Can we forget the titles, and the pomp and circumstance, and all the barriers we put up between real human connection and meet everyone at the human level? You're a human and I'm a human. We both want to be happy and fulfilled. Neither of us wants to suffer even a little bit. When we meet each other at this level, truthfulness comes easy in our speech and actions because we are meeting everyone the same as we would meet a cherished loved one.

Astaya (non-stealing), is the third *yama*. Like the first two *yama*, this one should be obvious to all of us, and yet we steal in conscious and unconscious ways, and in ways that we have convinced ourselves are harmless. I stole from just about every employer I ever worked for. If the till was over five dollars, that went in my pocket. I said to myself, "There, now the till is balanced. No one's the wiser, and I'm up five bucks." Or I would rationalize, "No one is going to miss this box of Sharpies. I'll just take these home." No one missed that box of markers or the five dollars, but I was planting seeds, seeds that would do me in later.

It seemed like every time I had two quarters to rub together, something would come along and take it; a random bill or unexpected car repair. Then I would get mad at the Universe. Every time I would get a little bit ahead, it would knock me back down.

And then there was the irony that, although I would steal, I had a hard time accepting gifts. Now I practice accepting with gratitude that which is offered to me in kindness, and not taking what is not mine. Also, we should not want things unnecessarily. The more we want, the more we will want, and the more we will feel a sense of lack. If we let this hunger go unchecked, it will become greed.

Now that we have the obvious ones out of the way, we come to *brahmancarya* (on the path of Brahman). In order to talk about *brahmacharya*, we first have to understand a couple of things. *Brahma* is the word for universal intelligence or God, if I may use that word. A Brahman is a priest.

As I said earlier, a young Brahman enters into the path of *brahmancarya* at the age of eight, and for twelve years, they are separated from their family. They do not engage in intimate relations with the opposite sex. They eat, sleep, do chores, and chant the *Vedas* over and over and over, hearing it from the lips of their teachers and repeating them until they are memorized perfectly.

In a broader sense, what are they doing? They're removing anything that could be a distraction from their spiritual practice, so that all of their energy and focus is devoted to one thing.

Patañjali laid out the monastic path, the path of the renunciate who has no family, no children, and no career. The message is clear; one should renounce everything and devote all energy to spiritual development. But what does *brahmacharya* mean to those of us who don't want to be monks?

Well, in order to understand that, we must understand

who we are. If we are not monks, then what are we? Do you have to be a monk to have a spiritual life? Is there another path? Yes. There is *tantra*.

Tantra yoga is the path of the householder. For a long time, the monk's path was the only path for yoga, but after many years, the ordinary, everyday people with jobs and homes and families desired a spiritual life too. This is the tradition they took, and this is where yoga went from a very narrow green chute of understanding and flowered into a wonderful truth that was available to anyone.

Most Westerners who have heard of *tantric yoga* associate it with sex. This is a very limited view of *tantric yoga*. Remember that *sānkhya* philosophy is dualistic; *puruṣa* and *prakṛti* (spirit and matter). Things are either spirit or material.

The method is to disengage from anything material and focus solely on the spiritual. While this method does work and is a viable path for many, *tantric yoga* finds a deeper truth that *puruṣa* and *prakṛti* are both ultimately Brahma when they take the original twenty-five *tattva* and expand it to the thirty-six *tattva*.

Everything is divine; spirit and material. Everything is God. One does not need to renounce the material world to know the divine; quite the opposite. The goal is to see the divine in everything, even things that are supposedly taboo or against normal cultural values of what is pure and divine, like sex or alcohol consumption, drug use, et cetera.

Anyone who has had sex with a partner where you are both in it for the other's pleasure and not your own will agree it is a truly divine experience. Going out, getting drunk, and singing with friends at the top of your lungs?

163

God is there.

I know it's a lot to understand, but for now, just know that if you are not renouncing the world, but rather engaging in it, while still pursuing a spiritual life, then you are practicing *tantra yoga*. *Tantra* comes from the root *"tan,"* which means to extend, to spread. *Tantra* means to weave. *Tantric* is the word for doctrine or text. Tantrika is the name for one who follows the path.

What does *brahmacharya* mean to us, then? I look at it this way: all relationships are essentially an exchange of energy. Our relationships are best when they are a mutual exchange, meaning all those involved both give and receive. Some relationships require more of our energy than others.

When we are young, we tend to have many friends because it only takes a small amount of energy to keep those friendships going and keep them healthy. Later on, we get a partner and, by definition, this relationship requires more of our energy, which translates into intimacy, because both of you are investing more. You wind up with someone who is closer to you, more important to you than just a friend.

It's not like you have limitless energy. So naturally, because you are investing more into your partner, you wind up dropping a couple of friends that were not benefiting you much. Later on, perhaps you get married. Marriage requires even more of your energy, and so you lose a couple more.

Marriage is unique in the sense that one has to take the long view on mutual exchange. When we marry someone, we are promising them that even if things get bad for a while, we're going to stick around. Hopefully, most of the time it is a fifty/fifty partnership, but when we are looking at a lifetime together, we understand that if our partner becomes depressed or ill, we will have to step up and give more for a while, and vice versa. Hopefully, over the course of a life together, both parties feel that it was mutually beneficial.

When people get divorced, they often say something like, "I just couldn't do it anymore." They have no more energy left to give. They gave so much for so long, without anything in return, that they literally can't give anymore. The relationship is not healthy, and so it ends.

If we have children, they require every ounce of our energy for at least the first ten years. In this decade, we lose all but our most important friendships, because we simply have no energy to invest in them. I think most parents feel like there is no limit to what they would give to/do for their children. We give them all of our energy with very little in return, even to the point where it is killing us. That is the nature of the relationship.

Then, of course, we also have a relationship with our career. It's a good relationship when we feel like we're getting paid enough, are not overworked, and still have time for our families and other passions. When we spend all of our time working and still can't make ends meet, it becomes draining.

There is one more relationship that we have—our relationship with the divine. This relationship is always beneficial. Whatever you put into it is miniscule in comparison to the dividends it will pay out in return. It is always a benefit to invest in your spiritual life, but you must first have the energy to invest. Even a little bit every day pays out. As my teacher told me, "All you have to do is take one step towards God, and God will come across the universe to meet you."

Brahmacharya for us could mean, "preserve your energy." Preserve your energy so that you have enough left over to invest in your yoga practice. You don't want your practice to become just one more thing on your to-do list. You don't want it to feel like a burden or an obligation. Don't waste energy on people or activities that constantly drain you. Your relationship with the divine, if you have the energy to invest in it, will never deplete you. It will always recharge you, because you are connecting to the source of all energy. This enhances all of your other relationships.

You could renounce the world and all other relationships and devote all of your energy to your spiritual practice. But is that really living? Personally, I would rather engage in the world responsibly, hopefully to the benefit of everyone who comes into contact with me.

Brahmacharya is about prioritizing where you spend your energy. For me, that is in the following order: family, career, and spiritual community. Your priorities will change throughout your life, but having a spiritual practice will help you be the best spouse, partner, employer, employee, parent, friend, son, daughter, etc., and to live in a state of peace and joy. Practice yoga not to get better at yoga, but to get better at living.

Aparigraha (non-grasping), is the fifth and final *yama*. It means: "do not cling to impermanent things or ideas." Everything that is has a beginning and an end. Everything is always changing. Nothing is permanent. Our Egos, our sense of I, was created to give us a sense of continuity. It gives us the illusion of permanence. After all, I was here yesterday and I'm here now. We take it as a given that we will be here tomorrow. This gives us a sense of security, albeit a false one.

But human beings need a sense of security, because the Universe is an entirely unsafe and insecure place. When faced with that Truth, we freak out. We go into survival mode. We are fearful and anxious. This makes us aggressive, tribalistic, territorial, and distrustful. When we feel safe, our human qualities come out. When we are calm and relaxed, we can be trusting, honest, compassionate, empathetic, and generous.

This was the original intent of government and religion; to give us a sense of security so that we can be humans, not animals. Sooner or later, this fraud, like all scams, breaks down. It never lasts. How could it? It is an illusion of safety, and it all starts with the ego.

The Ego accumulates and attaches to things and ideas that make it feel more solid, more tangible, more permanent. It seeks immortality, which we know is an impossibility. It can become obsessed with ideas like legacy, power, and influence, trying to create something that will endure once the body dies. Our greatest attachment is to our own life, and all of our fears stem from the fear of our own death.

That great unknown is terrifying, because there's no way of knowing it, and what we don't know, we fear. The Ego attaches itself to an identity in order to handle the unknown, but this causes a great deal of unnecessary suffering, if for some reason we lose that identity. For example, if I identify with my profession and I lose my job, then I will feel as though I have lost myself. If I identify as a husband and I lose my wife, then again, I am lost.

I never thought I would be a teacher of any kind, let alone a yoga teacher, but it has been more fulfilling than anything I've ever done in my life. Somewhere over the last ten or eleven years, I became attached to it. My ego started to say, "I am a yoga teacher."

When the coronavirus pandemic forced us all into lockdown, and my yoga studio sat empty for months, I tried to hold the community together through online classes. The fear of losing the yoga school and my attachment to it threw me off my balance.

For weeks, I fretted and worried. I had anxiety attacks for the first time ever in my life. I thought I was having a heart attack, and in a way, I was. I fell into bouts of depression that left me sitting in the shower, staring at the wall or emotionless in bed, escaping into video games to avoid my thoughts. My heart was breaking because of an attachment to an impermanent idea and a theoretical future that I was projecting. The unknown caused me great fear.

One afternoon, while lying in bed once again, staring at my phone, trying to avoid my thoughts, an epiphany cut through the fog like a beam of sunlight. I saw the source of my suffering for what it was. Once I could see it clearly, it was done, over. In a wave of calm, cooling comfort, I exhaled a shuddering breath and thought, "Fuck... *Īśvara praṇidhāna.*"

It is important to remember that *yama* may be social disciplines about the way we should interact with others, but the supreme realization through yoga is that there are no others. That is the illusion of duality. The experience is real, but under the surface is the Truth that all is one.

Balance is the fundamental principle of the Universe. When everything is in balance, all is one.

It is in the fluctuations of balance that everything exists as different things. Day is balanced by night, hot by cold etc. Every individual thing inherently seeks out a return to balance, for that is its original state. So how we treat "others" is ultimately how we are treating ourselves, thus creating equanimity in our lives.

Chapter Seventeen

The second spoke on the wheel of *aṣṭāṅga*, the eight-limb practice, is *niyama*. *Niyama* are the personal observances of the yogi. These things are observed daily, and there are five of them. *Śauca* is the first one, and it means "purity or cleanliness". Patañjali puts purity here in the traditional Brahmanical sense of the word, meaning abstinence from alcohol, rich foods, and sexual indulgence.

At one point in history, these ideas about purity were actually the tipping point that caused the householders to rebel against Brahmanic tradition and create the tantric path. As is often the case, change is messy. Just think of how awkward our physical bodies can be during adolescence. Before the change, the Brahmans had become corrupt, much like the Catholic church in the middle ages. They began to use their vast power and influence to lay down laws about purity that made life for the average householder inordinately complicated and difficult, so the householders began to do their own prayers and rituals.

One of the *śauca* rules that still exists to the present day is "one does not eat with the left hand". You use the left hand to wipe your bottom (not actually that poor of an idea at the time, considering the lack of running water and sanitation). It is because of the willingness to add so-called "impure" things into their rituals that *tantra* became known as the left-handed path.

Do we just throw out *śauca* then? No, we take a broader understanding of it. I prefer to use the cleanliness translation of the word. "*Śauca* is the first *niyama*," a teacher of mine would often say, as we were picking up to leave the room at the end of class. "A yogi should always leave a place at least as clean as the way they entered it."

It is such a beautiful way to go through the world. When you enter a space, do it cleanly, not just physically, but also mentally and emotionally. Don't mess things up. This refers to our houses, cars, and other personal spaces as well. Do you kick your shoes off haphazardly when you get home, or do you place them neatly? Do you make your bed in the morning, brush your teeth, and clean your nails and hair?

Śauca is about taking care with your actions and environment. A cluttered environment makes for a cluttered mind. Getting rid of and not collecting things we don't need or can't use creates space in our environment and in our heart-mind by eliminating attachments.

When things are going rough in my life, I often clean my house. It helps me clear my head and assert a sense of making a difference to my external circumstances. I may not like the way things are, but I can make things clean.

When I was in about third or fourth grade, I asked my father for help with my math homework. He said, "Sure, go wait in your room, and I'll be there in a minute." I was sitting at my desk, which is covered in books, drawings, colored pencils, schoolwork, and toys.

I was fiddling with an action figure when my dad

opened the door. He looked at my desk and then at me, and then back at my desk and said, "Well, I'm not surprised you're having trouble with your homework. You're surrounded by distraction. How do you expect to organize your thoughts when your workspace is a mess?"

The Truth of his words sunk in. I have always remembered this moment. When I think of the importance of *śauca*, it goes both ways. I am doing the inner work to make the outer better and making the outer clean and organized helps me do the inner work.

Santoṣa is the second *niyama*. *Santoṣa* means contentment. Contentment is the acceptance of others and one's own circumstances as they are. As I've been saying all along that we don't have to like it, but if we don't want to suffer, we cannot put ourselves at odds with what *is*. Acceptance brings contentment. Beliefs cause suffering.

Ram Das (Richard Albert) had a wonderful teaching where he explained, "When you go out into the woods and you look at the trees, you see all these different trees, and some of them are bent. You sort of understand that it didn't get enough light, and so it turned that way, and you don't get all emotional about it. You just allow it. The minute you get near humans, you lose all that, and you say, 'you are too this, or I am too that'. That judgment mind comes in. And so I practice turning people into trees, which means appreciating them just the way they are."

We can apply that, not just to people, but also to circumstances of our existence like when we are grieving the death of a loved one, especially if they were young or it happened unexpectedly. In our pain, caused by the attachment to impermanent things that we believed to be

172

permanent, it is easy for us to think their death was wrong. We believe that it shouldn't have been their time when it actually was their time. It is hard to accept that they lived their whole life.

This lack of acceptance turns our grief into suffering. Whereas if we accept circumstances as they are, we can grieve while being content with the time that we shared with them. BKS Iyngar, in his book *Light on Life*, says that he didn't cry at his wife's funeral. Not because he didn't love her, but because he was unattached and content.

Niyama three, four, and five are the practices of *kriyā yoga*. Which, as we already discussed are: *svādhyāya* (self-study), *tapas* (austerity), and *Īśvara praṇidhāna* (attunement to supreme consciousness).

After teacher training, I really truly began to practice *yama* and *niyama* in every moment of every day to the best of my ability. I made mistakes of course, but there are no mistakes. Mistakes are lessons. Did I fail? All the time. But I kept trying and am still trying. The journey has not ended.

Chapter Eighteen

The next spoke of the wheel of *aṣṭāṅga* (eight-limb path) is *asāna* (posture). This is the part most modern practitioners think of as yoga; the poses, the physical exercises. Although when Patañjali writes about *asana*, he is speaking of meditation posture. *Asāna* could also be translated as seat or throne.

Lotus pose, or *siddhāsana*, is the original yoga posture, and Patañjali tells us *"sthira sukham asanam."* The posture should be comfortable and steady. At this point in history, this was yoga. Sitting in concentration (*dhāraṇā*), that gives way to meditation (*dhyānā*), and meditation leads to absorption into spirit (*samādhi*).

It wasn't until much later, around the turn of the twentieth century, that yogis influenced by Western gymnastics and athletics fleshed out the practice of *asāna* into what we recognize today. Because the method was no longer to renounce the body and senses, tantric yogis began to study the body. It is because of their efforts that we have the chakra system of energy in the body, and the map of the *nadi* system (how energy flows in the body).

In the 1980s, Sri Dharma Mitra created the master chart of nine hundred and eight yoga *asāna* as a gift to his guru Yogi Gupta. He stopped at nine hundred and eight because eight is the infinity symbol if turned sideways.

The implication is that there is no limit to the postures we can create from the human form. We are still coming up with new ones all the time. Everything is always changing, including yoga.

Even though we have many more postures now than we used to, we can still apply Patañjali's teaching to them all. No matter how complicated the posture is, we work to be comfortable and steady, just as if we were sitting.

In line with the goal of liberation from suffering, we can begin at the physical level. Through regular balanced exercise, we can remove pain from the body. We can remove stress which becomes disease. We can clear restlessness from the body, which will make it easier to be still for the deeper practices of yoga. We condition the physical body so that *prāṇa* (vital life energy) can flow freely without restriction through it entirely. We cultivate a physical shell that can move and bend in any direction as easily as the energy contained within.

If one is in physical pain or ill all the time, this is a huge hurdle to freedom from suffering. Does this mean if one has a body incapable of doing exercise one cannot achieve liberation? Absolutely not, but it will certainly be easier if we can cultivate a healthy body.

Spoke four of the *aṣṭāṅga* is *prāṇayāma*. A surface translation could be *prāṇa* = breath, and *yāma* = discipline, so *prāṇayāma* is breath discipline, or breath control or breathing exercises.

But to really understand *prāṇayāma*, one must understand that *prāṇa* is more than just the air we breathe. It is that, but it is also the energy that runs the body, brain, and senses. Also, it is consciousness.

Consider for a moment that the first thing we do when we are born is draw breath in, and the last thing we will do in these bodies is exhale. So, from the beginning until the end, the breath is present. If we hold our breath for too long, we black out. We lose consciousness.

So, to a yogi there is no distinction between air, energy, and awareness. They are all *prāna*. So practice of *prānayāma* on the physical level is doing breathing exercises to make the lungs, heart, and circulatory system strong and healthy. On the energetic and mental levels, it is practicing the ability to move energy to various parts of the physical body through the *nadi* (energy channels) by focusing awareness on those places.

There are seventy-two thousand *nadi* that connect every part of the physical body to consciousness. *Nadi* are like a river and its tributaries. *Prāna* flows like water, but because *prāna* is awareness, it only flows to what we are aware of. Most humans do not have access to all seventy-two thousand *nadi*, because we haven't sent our awareness down them in a long time. So, they have become like a dry riverbed. The channel is still there, and we can revitalize it by flowing awareness through it.

Combining *asāna* practice with *prānayāma* is highly effective for this task. The posture is a tool that brings different areas of the body into awareness by causing sensation there. The sensation captivates the attention of awareness, and so *prāna* flows through the *nadi* to that place. You can feel this happening. The *prāna* removes the stress, and you can feel the sensation become less and eventually dissipate completely over time.

It would be easy to think that the posture causes the sensation, but the Truth is that we accumulate stress just by living, and we store it in the body. We carry it around unconsciously until it is so severe that it becomes pain. If we don't deal with it, it will become a "dis-ease," a sickness. Or before that happens, we do *asāna*. The *asāna* shows us where we are holding the stress, we become aware of it, *prāna* flows to it and heals it.

Doing *asāna* and *prānayāma* to me is about taking responsibility for the stress of your own existence and dealing with it in a healthy way. We bring our physical bodies into balance by allowing the life-giving power of awareness to flow into and through every nook and cranny of it. Then there is no pressure or strain on the energy body. Then the heart-mind begins to function properly. We become more emotionally balanced and stable. We can meet each new day fresh, without the accumulated weight of the previous days.

Which brings us to spoke five, *pratyahara*, or "withdrawal of the senses from the objects of their perceptions". Maybe a better way to say that would be turning off our sense perceptions. Imagine a turtle pulling its head back into its shell, or a rose blossom returning to a bud.

For most of the time each day that our eyes are open and we are awake, our awareness (which is our life energy, remember) is focused outward towards the world and interacting with it. You could think of your awareness like the beam of a flashlight. You are only aware of whatever you point the light at, and whatever you are aware of is receiving the energy of your awareness. Everything you are unaware of is in darkness. *Pratyahara* is turning the flashlight to point inwards. Illuminating and energizing different aspects of your inner experience.

Having now prepared and disciplined the body, energy, emotions, and senses, we can now bring awareness to the mental level.

Spokes six and seven are *dhāraṇā* (concentration) and *dhyānā* (meditation). What is the difference between concentration and meditation? Concentration is one-pointed focus on something external. Meditation is the same but focused inwardly. Awareness does not wander, and there is an absence of thought or internal dialog.

For example, one could light a candle and stare at the flame until the flame was the only thing in awareness. This would be concentration. If one then closed the eyes and pictured the flame in the mind, then this image would be the only thing in awareness. This is meditation. This may sound simple, but like most things in yoga, they sound simple, but the execution of it can be quite challenging.

Concentration becomes meditation, and meditation calms the fluctuations of the mind, bringing it to one point of awareness. When awareness then becomes absorbed into universal consciousness or immersion into spirit, we are back to where we started trying to get to in the first place, spoke eight, *samādhi*.

We have worked our way back through the *kośa* (layers of self) from gross to subtle. Reconnecting with our essential nature brings us back into alignment with Truth, ending ignorance, dragging us out of darkness, back into the light, and liberating us from suffering.

The Eight Limbs of Yoga are:

1. *Yama* – How you treat others
2. *Niyama* – How you treat yourself
3. *Asāna* – Physical postures
4. *Prānayāma* – Regulation of breath and life force
5. *Pratyahara* – Withdrawal of the senses from sensory objects
6. *Dhāraṇā* – Concentration
7. *Dhyānā* – Meditation
8. *Samādhi* – Absorption into spirit

As I explored yoga deeper, I really struggled with all the God and Lord talk. There was no doubt in my mind that the more I practiced yoga, the better I felt about life, myself, and others. Yoga had proven itself to me as a lifestyle. After years of being human and having no idea how to do that properly, it felt like I had found the user's manual, but I was still so resistant to any talk of the divine.

Did I have to believe in God? Surely that was just some archaic way of looking at things. Couldn't I just ignore all that stuff? Struggling with these questions, I sought out a new teacher who I felt understood the spiritual side of the practice more than most.

I had met and worked with her privately for a while, and it was through her that I learned of David Life and Sharon Gannon of *jivamukti yoga*. These people were "real yogis," I was told. "They lived it."

I was interested. They sounded like people from whom I would want to learn. I got the *jivamukti* book and read about their story and their view of yoga. They seemed like

179

There Is No Me

wild, artistic people; people I could relate to. When the opportunity to study with them for ten days in upstate New York presented itself, I went with three hundred others.

The beginning of our ten-day study crossed over with the final day of Bhakti Fest, a chanting festival which had been going on for three days prior to our arrival. This was intentional. Our ten days was to begin with twelve hours of chanting, which immediately threw me well out of my comfort zone.

I was familiar with several of the artists who would be leading the *kirtan* (group chant): Krishna Das, Jai Uttal, and several others. You might think that given my love for music, I would have been excited, but no, I was still too closed off and fearful. I'd never experienced a group chant, and I knew very little about mantra.

Any time I would ask someone about the meaning to what we were chanting, I would get answers like "It's not about the meaning, it's about the vibration." You have to feel it.

Mr. Logical found this answer unsatisfactory. I remember thinking that twelve hours of chanting was a little brainwashy. As I write that now, I have to chuckle a little, because it was a brainwashing, a cleansing of energies, but not in any kind of sinister way.

As I entered the temple on this occasion, I was greeted with a scene that my memory told me was some kind of mashup between a Grateful Dead concert and a worship service at my parents' church. This was a very confusing juxtaposition for me. I found a place near a wall and tried to disappear. I felt very awkward and out of place. I listened and watched for a while, but once it became apparent that we could come and go as we pleased and were not required to participate, I took off to my tent and went to bed.

During the next nine days, I learned a great deal and enjoyed my escape into the first experience of *sangha* (a spiritual community). It was a little utopian community. It was reminiscent of P.L.U.R. from rave culture, but clean and pure. There were people doing yoga, serving, and seeking quiet contemplation. Everyone was friendly and willing to engage in deep, meaningful conversation. Human connection was everywhere. Everything seemed in harmony with the environment.

It was autumn, and there was so much color and sun and crisp, clean air in the morning. It was wonderful, but I very much felt like an outsider; not because of anyone else's words or actions, but because of myself. I could not fully open myself up to it all. I wound up feeling like I was watching it all through the window of a moving train.

Until this retreat, I had thought of the eight limbs of yoga like a ladder to ascend, a recipe to follow. I believed that the *yama* and *niyama* came first, followed by the physical postures and breath work, which lead to concentration, which lead to meditation, and then finally to *samādhi*.

What I learned from David and Sharon was not to think of it linearly, because nothing is linear in actuality. At the end of the training, there was a Q&A period. I only had one question that I couldn't figure out. Why did we start every day with meditation, and then move to mantra and postures? That order didn't make sense to me. If the poses prepared the body for meditation, why meditate first? It felt like putting the eggs in the cake after it was cooked.

And so I asked them, "If *asāna* prepares the body for

meditation, then why do we sit silently at the beginning of class, and not at the end?" They laughed and looked at each other and then back at me. David replied with the question, "Didn't you practice *asāna* yesterday?"

I understood his meaning. I am not baking a cake. The eight limbs are not a recipe. All the work every day is connected and moving towards the same goal: liberation. This is when I started thinking of the eight limbs like the spokes on the wheel of a ship. All of them are simultaneously helping us to steer our ship to our destination, liberation.

As I drove out of the retreat center and headed back to my home, the first thing I saw was a giant illuminated sign for Exxon gas, and then the McDonald's arches. I sighed and shook my head. "This, in a nutshell, is everything that is wrong with our culture," I thought. I was inspired by my experience. I felt like I had found "real yoga", and I couldn't wait to share it with my students.

When I found hot power yoga, the yoga classes at the gym felt like they were missing something. Once I had found *jivamukti yoga*, hot yoga felt like it was missing pieces, too. *Jiva* means soul and *mukti* means liberation. Together, *jivamukti yoga* means "yoga to liberate your soul". And that's how this new yoga felt. I had found the Holy Grail, and I was bringing it back for everyone to drink from! I'm laughing as I write this. I hope you are laughing as you read it.

I began to start all of my classes with five minutes of silent sitting. I would come in, introduce myself, tell everyone to sit comfortably and close their eyes. I would set the timer for five minutes and then just sit there quietly with my eyes closed until it chimed. Then I would call for three ohms, tell them to open their eyes, and we would start our postures.

When forced to sit silently with their own thoughts for five minutes, people lost their minds. The owner of the studio was inundated by phone calls and emails telling her that they didn't like the new way I was teaching class. In just a couple of weeks, attendance in my class dropped to about a third of what it was previously. When Matthew told me he wanted to sit down and have a chat with me, I wasn't surprised.

The owner told me that whatever I was doing wasn't working and that I needed to go back to teaching the way I used to. I was angry, and like a petulant child, I decided to push back. I told them I would go back to teaching like I had before, but I needed to cut back on how many classes I was teaching. "It's taking up too much of my time on Saturday," I said arrogantly, like I was punishing them in some way.

I realized how silly I was being when I calmed down and looked at it clearly, and I learned an important lesson. We have to meet people where they are. The job of the teacher is to move the students towards the goal. So I went back to teaching the old way, and slowly, very slowly, moved towards what felt authentic. I changed my classes so gradually that nobody noticed it was happening.

It's funny to reflect back on this, because all of my classes begin with silent sitting now, and that is what the students expect. If I didn't do it, they would be confused. One must be consistent in their teachings, and change should happen gradually, because what you teach attracts the student who wants to learn that. If what one is offering is all over the place, you will get nowhere, because there is no opportunity to build trust. Trust is relationship, and in the teacher/student relationship, it is everything.

It was right around this time that my relationship with Matthew began to fall apart for the third and final time. When they found a teacher to replace me on Saturdays, I decided to take the class. In my mind, I thought it would be good to show my support for the new teacher.

In hindsight, I know that I was not seeing clearly. It was weird and awkward for the new teacher and the students to have me there. I set up a mat for myself and one next to me for Matthew. When he entered the room, he deliberately avoided me, and it was obvious. I understood I had made a mistake, but why not just tell me later? Why disrespect me in front of everyone?

Matthew was a very hard person to be friends with, and I had hung on longer than most. He was judgmental and held everyone he interacted with to a very high standard. We met for coffee, and at some point in the conversation, he made a comment about me "riding on his coattails." It was like a slap in the face.

In anger, I told him I was "looking for a friend, not a teacher," and that "even if I did want a teacher, it wouldn't be him." I told him that if he wanted to "hang out, smoke some weed, and play video games, then to give me a call, but otherwise, I'm not interested."

As I left the coffee shop and walked to my car, I knew in my heart that our friendship was over. I will always love him. He was a brother, a friend, and a mentor, and even though we have not spoken any meaningful words to each other in a decade, I still think of him, most of the time fondly. I saw us as equals, but he wanted to be my superior.

I was at a point in my yoga where I was feeling the need to stand on my own two feet. I kept thinking, "I need to go it alone for a while, without anyone to lean on when things get tough. I need to see if I can do this."

From that moment forward, I walked the path of yoga very much alone for a long time.

I've never let up on my studies. It is important to stay curious. One must work to find inspiration. When walking alone, it can be hard at times to stay motivated. That is why community is so important on the journey.

Chapter Nineteen

The *Bhagavad Gita* is probably the most famous of the yoga texts. It is one section of a much larger text called the *Mahābhārata* epic. I'm not going to give an in-depth analysis of the *Gita* here. I mainly want to talk about the concept of *karma yoga*. The *Mahābhārata* tells the tale of a king who dies, and the struggle for the throne between his sons and his nephews. It all comes to a head in a giant battle. The *Gita* is the story that takes place just before the battle starts.

The two armies are lined up on opposite sides of the battlefield, waiting to charge. Banners are flying in the wind, and conch shells are being blown like trumpets. Arjuna, one of the king's sons, tells his charioteer Kṛsnā to drive him out into the middle of the field.

Once he arrives, he throws down his bow and breaks down, having a crisis of conscience. Arjuna doesn't want war. He doesn't want to kill his cousins, uncle, and teacher. He feels that even if he and his brothers prove victorious, they will still lose. He believes it would be better to not fight and to become a beggar than to kill one's own family.

Kṛsnā's response is some of the most beautiful spiritual wisdom ever expounded into writing. He explains to Arjuna that yoga is about balance, and that we all have a part to play in the great cosmic game. Kṛsnā tells him that he is a warrior, and that these men are evil. It is Arjuna's duty to pick up his bow and fight.

Kṛsnā goes on to say that he wants to convey a way of yoga that has been forgotten, *karma yoga*. *Karma yoga* is a concept of renunciation, but one need not renounce the world and all action as the ascetics do. One only needs to renounce the fruit of one's actions. Do your duty (*dharma*), fulfill your role in the game, and come what may from your actions. We may like or not like what results, but that is of no concern to us, or should not be, anyway.

Our concern is to fulfill our role and help the universe weave the pattern of life. A selfish action incurs karma. It causes a flaw in the pattern that must be mended. A selfless action, that works for the benefit of all, is karma free, for it serves the ultimate purpose of completing the tapestry. In my case, it meant adopting a baby.

After Angela and I had moved into our own place, my father and I would meet for breakfast to talk a couple of times a month, so when he called and asked me to meet him for breakfast, it was nothing out of the ordinary.

When I arrived, it was clear that he was anxious. After dancing around it for a while, he finally told me that the youngest of my three sisters was six months pregnant. I thought she had looked like she had put on some weight at Thanksgiving, but she was mostly hiding it under a big sweatshirt.

My parents had adopted her and one of my other sisters after fostering them for many years. She was only seventeen and still a minor, which gave my parents all the control. I knew she didn't have a whole lot of options. She was not ready to be a mom. My parents were getting too old to raise another baby, and given their beliefs about abortion, well, abortion was not an option. It was too late for that. This person was coming into the world, and adoption was my sister's only option.

My conscience screamed at me! "Everyone in this situation is suffering!" My parents, my sister, and the unborn child. It was all suffering. And all I could see is the one thing I could do that would end all of the suffering and turn it into joy. My inner voice spoke again, "You always said that this is the only way you would become a parent." There was only one right choice here, and I knew what it was. I didn't say anything to my dad at that moment. I went home and told Angela what was going on.

With a cheeky grin on my face, I asked Angela, "Do you want to adopt a baby?" I was hoping she would say no and give me a way out of it. She looked at me intensely without a trace of sarcasm and said as deliberately and sincerely as she could, "Yes. Yes, I do." That was it.

We spoke with my parents and my sister and told them we wanted to adopt the baby and with that, we shifted the suffering to joy. Baby Penelopi entered the world on April 4th, 2011 at about ten p.m.

Most people get nine months to prepare for a child. We got three. It was a whirlwind of painting, preparation, anticipation, and excitement. Penelopi is about to turn ten as I write this. She's a force of nature. We've always been upfront with her about her origins. We tell her that she is our daughter, and that the only way she could get to us was through my sister.

Parenting challenges us all to become our best selves. And in order to do that, we have to face our own *saṃskāra* (mental imprints). Being Penelopi's father is the single greatest role I've had in life. She's my greatest teacher and always challenges me. I look forward to knowing the woman she becomes.

Karma yoga ends the suffering of oneself and those around oneself. We all must act, so when that moment comes, choose for the good of all involved. Doing what your heart-mind and senses are telling you is the right choice. I have never found myself regretting when I choose to act from the higher self. Only when I act in my own interests, selfishly, do I wind up not liking the outcome.

Circumstances at the trombone shop continued to decline. The great recession of 2008 had been hard on the business, and for years after, the management did a horrible job managing cash flow. More and more often, we had to wait to cash our paychecks, and for longer and longer periods of time.

I was tired of the stress it caused me. I was tired of being around all these negative people all the time. I was tired of the way I felt when I was there. I was tired. I had no energy left to give to the relationship.

The straw that broke my back was finding out that they had let the workman's comp insurance lapse. Not only was that illegal, but it was an incredibly dangerous job. One guy had already lost a finger. Honestly, I'm surprised there were not more injuries. The fact that there weren't is only a testament to our skills, not the safety of the procedures.

I had fumed all day, not saying anything, and at the end of the day, I boiled over and found the foreman. I told him that I knew about the workman's comp insurance. "How could you let that happen? You know this is wrong," jabbing my finger in his face.

I went home. I knew I was done there. It was over. I considered just not going back, but something inside me said, "Just go in and see it through to the end. Don't run away."

So I did.

When the owner showed up, he walked up and said, "I want to see you in my office." I told him "I'm really not interested in anything you have to say." He was a liar and a manipulator. I knew if I went in there, he would just lie to me. He said, "Then you might as well just get out of here." And I said, "Okay." I left. Seven years in purgatory was over.

I had reaped the seeds of my old ways while planting the garden I wanted for the future. It was a bumpy transition. I had just walked away from half my income, and I had a mortgage and a two-year-old.

Eventually, I was able to teach enough classes to support my family, but barely. I was teaching hundreds of people a week, running retreats and teacher trainings, but it didn't matter. Finances were always tight, and any unexpected expenses were putting us into debt. Clearly, something had to change.

I realized that if I was going to be able to support my family teaching yoga, it was only going to be if I had my own place, but I was barely making ends meet. How was I going to get the money to start a yoga school?

That is what I wanted; a school, not a studio. Thinking about my ten days with *jivamukti yoga*, I wanted a real *sangha* (community) of people who wanted to learn yoga as a lifestyle and not just an exercise routine. Real seekers, who would do the work. I wanted to watch people transform their lives, once given the knowledge and space to do so.

When my mother's father passed away, my grandmother moved in with my parents. My grandmother was ninety-five at this point, and her care was taking up more and more of my mother's time. She had very little freedom.

My father suggested that Angela and I sell our house and move back into the apartment rent free. We could help them care for my grandmother and save up to start my yoga school. It wasn't what I wanted to do, but it was the best option we had.

So, Angela, Penelopi, and I have been living there ever since. My grandmother lived to be ninety-nine, and Angela cared for her like her own grandmother right up until the end.

My mom called as we were returning from the grocery store. "She's gone," my mom said. "I'll be right there, Mom," I said. She had lived a long life, and it was increasingly uncomfortable for her at the end. I was glad she was free, but I was sad for my mother.

A couple of years after that, Angela and I would open Burning Wheel Yoga School, but we didn't get there how you might think.

Chapter Twenty

I had come to a point where I felt I couldn't avoid *bhakti yoga* any longer. *Bhakti* means devotion. The principal practice of a Bhakta (one who practices *bhakti yoga*) is mantra. Mantra is a combination of "*man*", meaning mind, and "*tra*", meaning vehicle or transport.

Kirtan means narrating and reciting. It is a group chanting and storytelling session. Bhakta yogis simply want to worship the divine. They want a personal relationship with their *iṣṭa-devatā* which means one's favorite deity or personification of the divine. Some prefer the quality of a wise father figure, like the Jewish God. Some prefer to connect with the divine as the mother. Some want to know the divine the way a mother would love a child, and others may want to be the best friend or lover of the divine. All *iṣṭa-devatā* are just aspects of Brahma, the divine source, or universal consciousness.

This whole notion of devotion has always rubbed against my need to understand. I don't want to just blindly worship some limited notion of the divine. I want to comprehend the divine. My *iṣṭa-devatā* is the universe itself.

When I try to limit it to one form or aspect, it loses all of its awesomeness for me. When I think of the infinite void of nothingness and that within that is the potential for everything, I feel the power of the divine. I think of the quantum field that exists in every atom around the nucleus where the electron is everywhere and nowhere until we look for it, and this connects me to the divine. I think about the fact that if the electron were only one degree hotter or colder, than intelligent life would not exist in this universe. And the precision of that screams divine intelligence to me.

In Thomas Ashley-Farrand's book, *Mantra: Sacred Words of Power*, he explains how, if we go small enough, below the subatomic level, everything is waves of energy. Sanskrit mantra is about making a particular vibration or sound, and this sound is energy. Through the use of these energies, we can affect the circumstances of our existence by attracting or repelling other energies.

At one point in the book, he challenges the reader to take up a mantra for forty days and see what happens. He states that you don't have to believe for it to work. You can be completely skeptical. It works because that's what it does. He says you could go to the top of the empire state building and tell yourself gravity isn't real, but if you step off, you are still going to fall.

It is the same with mantra. Sacred words of power indeed, magic words. I always feel like I'm doing a magic spell when I chant a mantra. I chose a simple *Gaṇeśa Bīja* mantra and decided to commit to chanting it for a year. Gaṇeśa is the uniter of the groups (*guṇa*) and the remover of obstacles. He's depicted with four arms and the head of an elephant. The mantra is: *Oṃ gaṃ gaṇapataye namaha.*

I chose this mantra, because I felt as though there were still so many obstacles between me and my yoga school. The biggest of which was still funding. We had been living with my parents for four years at this point, and we had only succeeded in crawling out of debt and getting back to zero. We had not saved anything yet. I didn't think the mantra would work, but I also had nothing to lose, so I decided to go all in.

I threw out my television and couch to be replaced by meditation cushions and a low table, upon which I made a small shrine with some pictures of my teachers, candles, incense, and of course, a small statue of Gaṇeśa that I had purchased years earlier at the *jivamukti* retreat as a gift for Angela.

Thomas Ashley-Farrand proposes two ways to work with mantra. The first is to sit once a day with a *mālā* (rosary) and repeat the mantra one hundred and eight times, or you can repeat the mantra all day long whenever you can, both mentally and out loud when you feel comfortable doing so. I committed to doing both.

It's funny. I really didn't think it would work. Bhakta will tell you that there are two types of Bhakta; those who chant to receive some sort of boon from the divine, and those who chant simply because they love the divine and want to spend time in its presence. The latter is held in higher esteem.

I was most certainly the former, but I didn't care. This was an experiment to me. I was after the Truth. Part of me was hoping it wouldn't work, proving, once again, that God wasn't real. The other part of me really wanted a yoga school and was hoping it would work.

So I began chanting in the shower, "*Oṃ gaṃ gaṇapataye namaha*," and then silently when I was brushing my teeth. I chanted while making the coffee, and then I would chant on my forty-five-minute drive to work. I chanted while waiting for the students to arrive. I would sit with my *mālā* and chant.

All day, every day, I was chanting internally or audibly. I was repeating the mantra so much that I would wake up in the middle of the night and the mantra would still be running in my mind.

One night, about six months into my practice of mantra, I sat down in front of my shrine and lit the candles. It was about ten thirty p.m. on a warm summer night. The door to the outside was open, and it was raining gently. I could hear the pat, pat, pat of the raindrops, and I began to recite the mantra. After a few recitations, I decided I should just say it internally as Angela and Penelopi were already sleeping, and I didn't want to disturb them. I closed my eyes and took the mantra inside.

I started to feel the rhythm and the vibration of the sound, and my body began rocking to the rhythm. This had never happened before. Honestly, I felt pretty silly about it, but then something inside said, "Just go with it." So I did.

I relaxed into the rhythm and let my body move to it slowly. The rhythm of the raindrops joined the rhythm of the mantra and then the sound of the raindrops transformed into the sound of big hide-skin George of the Jungle drums!

My rational brain thought, "What is going on here?" But something deeper, call it my heart or soul, relaxed into the experience. As I relaxed, the mantra, the rain, and the drums were joined by massive horn blasts every time the mantra would repeat. It was a symphony. Behind my closed eyelids, a kaleidoscope of *maṇḍala* (circle) appeared in the

195

most vibrant colors and as bright as the sun, and every time the horns would blow, there would be a fan of elephant trunks.

My rational mind observed in stunned silence. I sat in awe and wonder, watching and listening for I don't know how long. It built into a massive crescendo of cacophonous sound and then slowly began to fade out, little by little, softer and softer, with every repetition, until once again, there I was sitting, listening to the pat, pat, pat of raindrops on the leaves. I opened my eyes to the image of the Gaṇeśa statue bathed in the warm glow of candlelight. Maybe it was the flicker of the candles playing tricks on my eyes, but I swear that statue was smirking at me. Something in me said, "Did I just meet Gaṇeśa?"

I wasn't quite sure what to do with what had just happened, so I went to bed, but every part of me was in agreement that what had just happened was real. There was no question, even from Mr. Logical. One might think that after this experience, my *iṣṭa-devatā* would be Gaṇeśa, but I prefer the Truth that Gaṇeśa is only one facet of the divine. The whole of it is so massive that a human can't ever hold it in awareness. It's the vastness of it that makes me feel it.

One might also think that after this, I would no longer question the validity of the divine or the powers of *bhakti yoga*, but this was just the moment when the seed was planted, it would take time and nurturing to flower. I continued to chant all day, every day. It got to a point where I felt like I was the mantra; like every atom in my body was vibrating with it.

My experience is that insight and epiphany all happen in a flash. They are instantaneous. The Truth just hits you. It's like a punch into you that plants a seed. I'm always left feeling a bit dazed and confused by the experience as I stumble back into ordinary, everyday life.

The effects of those moments, however, take shape gradually. It takes time and nurturing for those things to grow into our thoughts and actions.

I'd had one other experience that was similar, when the truth of *Advaita Vedānta* (non-dualism) hit me for the first time; not just intellectually, but viscerally. *Advaita Vedānta* to me is the crown jewel of yoga philosophy.

I think of the *Veda* like a bulb in the ground. The *Sāṇkhya Karika*, the *Yoga Sutrā*, and the *Gita* are like a big, green shoot that grows out of that bulb. *Advaita Vedānta* is a big, beautiful flower that blossoms from that stem.

Advaita Vedānta means non-duality and refers to the concept that Brahma (universal intelligence) is everything. Before *Advaita Vedānta*, remember, yoga philosophy was dualistic. But with the evolution of *tantric yoga*, it became non-dualistic. Everything is Brahma. Everything; you, me, the stars, love, darkness, even a piece of trash laying in the sewer, and the sewer itself.

Furthermore, it states that the true self, the *atman*, is not different from Brahma. Human consciousness is universal consciousness. There's no difference. Well, I had understood this as an idea for a while, but I didn't really comprehend it until the Truth of it hit me one day.

197

This was back when I had the little A-frame house and I was standing on the little balcony on the back of the house, up at its peak. I enjoyed smoking up there and thinking.

One day in the late afternoon, I was looking up at the sky thinking about God, and I thought, "Why do you always look up when you think about God?"

So I looked down at my backyard below me, and there was this giant pine tree, easily thirty feet tall. There was about six to eight feet of trunk at the bottom, and then the branches.

Because of the time of day and the angle at which the sun was hitting the tree trunk. It was divided exactly in half, half illuminated by the sun and half in darkness. As I stared at this tree, I thought, "Is God the light or the dark?"

And then the Truth hit me. Wham! It's both. It's up there and it's down here. It's the darkness and the light. It's out there and… it's… IN ME!

And for the first time in a long time, I could feel divinity in my body and understand it with my mind. What's great about that is the experience makes it tangible. Once we have experienced it, we don't have to believe it. It's real.

I continued my mantra practice, every day, all day, and about ten months in, something happened. I had been teaching at three different studios, all owned by the same people, and, due to some health issues and staffing problems, the owners made the decision to close one of the locations.

Angela and I thought, "This is the moment." If we were going to start our own school, this seemed like the right time, but how would we fund it?

We set to writing a solid business plan and began looking for a good location. We met with a construction company and came up with the plan to build our yoga school. The price tag was high. We were willing to take on the debt, but, try as we might, we couldn't get a loan as a brand-new business. And we had no collateral to speak of.

One day, I was sharing our plans with the owner of the studio that had just closed, and she suggested that we reopen their location. I was stunned. What an act of selflessness.

"You'd be okay with that?" I asked.

"Will you keep teaching for me?" she asked.

"Yes, of course," I replied.

"It's already built out as a yoga studio, and I know the landlord is trying to get someone else in there. I'd rather see it in the hands of you and Angela than someone else," she explained.

So, we spoke with the landlord and worked out a lease with no construction necessary. All we had to do was pay first and last month's rent. It was as easy as renting an apartment!

Part of the reason that I left the trombone shop was because I knew my time there was coming to an end. The yoga studio owners were already in the process of building a new third location, and I knew that when it opened, I would have enough classes to make up the lost income. I didn't know how it was all going to work out, but the Universe did.

You would think that after meeting Gaṇeśa and removing all the obstacles and chanting my way into my own yoga school that I would have had a moment of reconciliation, but I still wasn't quite ready for that. I finally had my yoga school, and there was work to do. There was plenty to keep me busy and distracted from the Truth.

Chapter Twenty-One

When I had asked Angela to marry me, I hadn't done the most romantic job. Opening the studio felt like another momentous step in our journey together, and it was an opportunity to redeem myself, so I went out and got a ring box and put the keys to the studio inside.

When I arrived home, I got down on one knee in front of Angela and asked, "Would you like to go into business with me?" I opened the ring box and presented her with the keys. She understood the gesture and laughed, saying, "Yes, of course I will!"

We spent the next month cleaning, painting and decorating the space. The school was going to be an extension of our home, and the *sangha* (community) there would be an extension of our family. We moved the shrine that had sat in our home for the last year into the practice space, and on October 1st, 2017, we opened the doors, and Burning Wheel Yoga School was born.

It was slow at first, but it gradually gained traction and momentum. It has been a delight and a treasure. It gives me great joy to watch people take the teachings of yoga, try them, put them to the test, and transform their lives.

I was speaking with one of them recently, and she said to me, "You changed my life."

I thanked her and replied, "I didn't. You did! All I did was give you the knowledge that was taught to me. You used the knowledge and did the work. You changed your life."

Her review on our Facebook page says it all, "Not a yoga workout kind of place. No shade on those, but a great place to breathe and work one's body through the poses, all while developing greater spirituality and oneness with the universe."

By January of 2020, we were poised to have a busy year. I was preparing to leave the studio where I had been working for a decade to solely focus on Burning Wheel and to spend more time with my family.

My father gave me some sage advice, as he does from time to time. He said, "Everyone I know who has become successful in life had to sacrifice something to get there." It had indeed been a long three years, but I was the most content I had ever felt. I experienced the equanimity that yogis often speak of. I felt balance in all things, and I was able to flow with the inevitable ups and downs of life with grace and ease. All the while, though, I knew it wouldn't last. Nothing lasts forever. Everything changes, and I was waiting for the thing that would come along and throw me off balance.

My parents had been snowbirds for years, retreating to Florida after the holidays to avoid the coldest months of the year. Angela, Penelopi, and I had never been down to visit them before, so when my parents urged us to take a break, we decided to book a trip to Universal Studios, Orlando. We were all very excited to experience the Harry Potter world there.

As we left on our trip, talk of the Coronavirus was starting to ramp up. The media was urging everyone to wash their hands and avoid touching their faces. This made for light crowds at the theme park, and we had a fun three days, but as we were leaving for the airport on the last day, we heard on the radio that they were closing the theme parks in Orlando.

I was watching online as one yoga studio after another closed their doors and switched to online classes. This was the moment where I lost my balance and fell. I didn't know what to do. Should I do as everyone else and close? In the end, I decided to teach all the classes myself and wait for an official word from the governor. Two days later, we were told to shut down, and I spiraled out.

While all of this was happening, I was right in the middle of a three-hundred-hour training in yoga philosophy that had started in September. As part of this program, we had monthly sessions with a mentor. I liked my mentor Mary from the first time an F-bomb slipped out of her mouth.

We were studying *bhakti yoga*, and I was doing my usual thing and expressing my dissatisfaction with *bhakti*. "Who needs devotion? *Jñāna* (knowledge) *yoga* is the best yoga! Yoga through knowledge, NOT devotion. I need to understand, not blindly follow," I protested.

I love teachers who ask you questions that lead you to the Truth, rather than telling it to you. Mary did this for me, and I love her for it.

She said, "You are devoted to your yoga practice, are you not?"

"Yes," I replied.

"And what about your family? Are you devoted to your family?"

"Well, yes, of course," I said.

"What's the problem with devotion, then?" she pressed.

Wham. There it was, I had walked right into it, like a glass door that I couldn't see.

What is the problem with devotion? Why is there this invisible barrier? These questions would just hang there with all the worry, fear, anxiety, depression, and heartache that I was going through as two weeks of lockdowns became four, and a month became two, and then three.

Finally, I saw the cause of my suffering: my attachment to Burning Wheel Yoga School.

I had nowhere left to run. I couldn't avoid it any longer. "*Īśvara praṇidhāna*," I whispered to myself. Surrender to the Lord. Oh, it just felt so oppressive, when you say it like that! It sounded like "submit to your master, slave," but what it really means is to let go of the things that are beyond your control. This situation was out of my control. There was nothing I could do about it, so I had to make peace with it. I had to surrender.

I had so many questions. What, in fact, am I surrendering to? Why could I be devoted to my practice and to my family, but not to God? Why does it feel so different? I sat with these questions until I began to see things clearly. My devotion to my practice and my family was motivated by memories that I had labeled as "pleasure." My practice and my family made me feel good.

In contrast, all the memories I had that were associated with devotion to God, I had labeled "pain." My devotion to

God as a child had come from obligation. It's what I was told to do.

I didn't know anything different. That devotion had caused me to experience ridicule and rejection, and ultimately, it ended in disillusion and heartbreak. Every time I thought about devotion to God, it was like a bad taste in my mouth. Now I understood I needed to resolve it logically.

So logically, "Is God real?" I asked myself. "Obviously, I'm not wondering if there is a man with a big white beard who lives in the sky and judges me. So what then am I asking? Is the Universe intelligent?" *Īśvara praṇidhāna* means devotion to the divine ideal. If I was going to be devoted to it, I needed to know that it is intelligent.

Saṇkhyā teaches us that there are three ways to gain right cognition: direct observation, inference, and valid testimony from one who knows. Ideally, we want consensus between the three. The classic Indian example of this is the saying, "Where there is smoke, there is fire." I have directly observed this, and others have experienced this to be true also. If I see smoke rising from a distant hill, I can rightly infer that there is fire on the hill, even though I can't see the fire.

Saṇkhyā goes on to point out that like produces like, and the cause is always visible in the effect it creates.

Alan Watts explains it like this: an apple tree produces apples, and within each apple are seeds. Inside each seed is the potential for another tree. The apple tree is the cause, and the apple is the effect. The apple tree apples. That's what it does.

What if we apply the same logic to the bigger question

that I am asking, "Is the universe intelligent?" The universe is the cause of everything. You and I are effects of the universe. Therefore, if I am intelligent, then the universe must be intelligent as well.

I sat with my mouth hanging open and wondered, "Could it really be that simple?" The simplicity of it does scream TRUTH, doesn't it? Do you feel the Truth in those words, dear reader? The Universe peoples, and within that effect is the seed; consciousness, *puruṣa*, *shiva*, whatever you want to call it. It is there.

I had come to the conclusion that the universe is intelligent, and that what I am surrendering to, or devoting myself to, is that supreme intelligence. But what about the things that are beyond my control or understanding? Why are they beyond my control? Why can't I understand?

I sat down, as I often do, and closed my eyes. I disentangled my awareness from the thought process by focusing on the sensations of breathing until my mind became calm and quiet. I pictured a pool of still water with a clear, clean surface, like a mirror.

I asked a question, like dropping a pebble into the pool, and I watched the ripples spread out across the surface of the water like the fluctuations of my thoughts. And then, when the water was still again, my mind was still again.

I dropped the question again. Over and over again, I dropped the question and watched the ripples, sometimes fast and sometimes slow. Eventually, understanding came up from the bottom of the pool, or, in other words, an insight came to me from collective consciousness. Things came into focus, and I could see it clearly.

What became clear was that it is a problem of scale and

perspective. I am intelligent, and so the universe is intelligent. That is clear. The universe is vast, which means it has an equally massive perspective. It can see everything.

I, on the other hand, am incredibly tiny in comparison, which gives me a very limited perspective. I can only see my little microcosm, my reality. There is no way I can ever understand everything. Some things are just unknowable, and that's okay. That's why we surrender to what we can't control. What we *can* understand is that if we could see the perspective of the universe, it would all make perfect sense.

I think about it like a painting by Georges Seurat, He created a style of painting known as pointillism. He used tiny dots of color to create a picture, like pixels before computers. The human perspective is like looking at a Seurat painting with your nose pressed to the glass. All you can see are a bunch of random, colored dots. It looks like chaos. There's no form or shape.

The Universal perspective is about ten paces back. The Universe can see the dots coalesce into shape and form, and ultimately a scene. It can see the whole picture.

There have been moments when I have felt like all of a sudden I was two paces back. I was not far enough to see the whole picture, but just far enough to know that there was a picture.

What I am doing when I am surrendering is using my free will to align my actions to serving the Universe's grand purpose, the divine ideal, even though I can't see what that is. I'm surrendering my fear, worry, anxiety, and all the things we experience when trying to control what we can't and don't understand.

So, I threw up my arms and said, "Okay, Universe, I

will continue to teach others about yoga whenever I can, however I can, as long as I'm breathing. And I can see that this is not dependent on Burning Wheel Yoga School existing or dependent upon yoga teaching being my occupation. But if our school is going to survive this pandemic, please give me the direction I need. I'm willing to do the work, but I don't know what to do."

It's been a year now. We are still here. In fact, I'm sitting at the front desk writing this right now, waiting for you to show up.

I know that everything happens for a reason. There are no such things as accidents or mistakes. There's no good luck or bad luck. The Universe is not for me or against me. I am the Universe. It's not about faith or belief. I have seen enough to trust that which I have not yet seen. I can see the smoke, so I know there is fire.

I came home one night, and as usual, Angela asked me how I was doing. I hit her with my best John Coffey voice and said his line from The Green Mile, "I'm tired, boss."

Mostly, I was tired of people being ugly to each other. I was tired of all the pain I was witnessing in the world every day. The pandemic was still raging. There were wildfires everywhere, protests and riots because of police brutality, and of course, the ongoing political divide.

She looked at me the way she always has and said, "I know that all you want to do is help people."

It's true. I suffer every day not because I'm in conflict with Truth, but because I know that things are the way they are, because *we* are the way *we* are. The world doesn't have problems. Humans have unresolved inner conflicts that we project onto the world.

For as long as there has been human civilization, we have been complaining about the same problems: war, poverty, inequality, injustice. We make these problems because of fear and our need for security. We create ego, government, nationality, political affiliation, race, gender, sexual orientation, and religion. They divide us further.

Krishnamurti said, "When you call yourself an American or a Muslim or a Christian or a European or anything else, you are being violent. Do you see why it's violent? Because you are separating yourself from the rest of the human race. When you separate yourself by beliefs, by nationality, by tradition, it breeds violence. So, a person who is seeking to understand violence does not belong to any country or any religion or any political party. They're concerned with the total understanding of mankind." There must be two for friction, which is conflict. If we are all one, then there can be no friction.

The world is always changing, and we influence that change. As Gandhi said, "We must be the change we want to see in the world." The alternative is to continue on the way we have for millennia, complaining about the same old problems.

Alan Watts said, "We suffer because we take seriously what the gods made for fun." I find that rings True. As long as I view the world through my limited perspective, it's all so serious. But the moment I take a couple steps back, it all becomes so silly.

For example, one day when Penelopi was three or four, she demanded a smoothie. She had been needy all day. Every five seconds, it was Daddy this and Daddy that, and I was becoming tired and frustrated. I poured some frozen blueberries into the blender and one blueberry bounced off the rim and rolled across the floor, leaving a trail of blue dots. I rolled my eyes and thought, "Great. Now I have to clean that up."

As I put the bag of blueberries down on the counter and turned around to clean up the one blueberry, the entire bag tipped over and a waterfall of blueberries cascaded onto the floor, rolling everywhere. I wanted to scream. I wanted to rage.

And then a voice inside me said, "Oh, come off it. If you were watching this happen on TV, you would think it was hilarious." And that was True. The whole scene was comical. So I sat down on the floor and laughed.

As I sat there laughing, I recalled a memory from when I was about ten years old. I was over at a friend's house. We were on the couch, watching TV. My friend's father was a big, round man with a big mustache. He looked like a walrus. He came walking through the room and stubbed his toe on the coffee table. We all heard the crunch; he had definitely broken a toe. I expected him to yell and scream or cry, but he sat down holding his foot in his hand, opened his mouth and let out a big belly laugh.

Confused, I asked him, "Did you just break your toe?"

Through laughter he replied, "I think so."

"Why are you laughing?" I asked.

"You either gotta laugh or cry, and I would rather laugh," he replied.

I think that True balance is when we can hold everything that is beautiful in one hand and everything that is ugly in the other, and comprehend that they are one whole, not opposite forces fighting each other. They are but polarities that work in concert to create. It is then that we experience *ānanda*, which means eternal bliss. That feeling when you're so happy or something is so beautiful that you cry.

Bill Hicks reminded us that, "The world is like a ride at an amusement park, and when you choose to go on it, you think it's real, because that's how powerful your mind is. The ride goes up and down, and around and around. It has thrills and chills, and it's brightly colored and loud, and it's fun for a while. Many people have been on the ride a long time and begin to wonder, is this real or is it just a ride? Other people have remembered, and they come back to us and say, 'Hey, don't worry. Don't be afraid ever, because this is just a ride'."

I love roller coasters. There's something so Zen about strapping in and surrendering to the ride.

When we went to Universal Studios, Orlando, there was a new roller coaster called Hagrid's Motorbike Adventure. If you like roller coasters, you may want to skip this part, because I'm going to ruin the surprise for you.

It's a two-person car shaped like Hagrid's motorcycle and sidecar (Hagrid is a character from the Harry Potter books). The ride does a couple of loops and a corkscrew, and at the end of the track, it stops and goes backwards through everything again. When you arrive back at the start, thinking the ride is over, the car suddenly and without warning drops twenty vertical feet.

The fall caught me so unaware, and the surprise made me laugh with joy! When the ground falls out from underneath me in life, I remember this ride, and I remember that this life is just a ride. It's the unexpected that makes life lively, and I would much rather laugh than cry.

When Angela said that she knew that all I wanted to do was help people, I thought of all these things. Then she said, "I know it's all inside you." She put her hand on my chest and said, "Write it down." Something about her words pierced my heart as surely as an arrow. And I said, "Okay, I will write it." And then I closed my eyes and fell asleep.

What then of these three questions that have been a thorn in my mind?

Remember when I said that the answer was in the word "I"? Where did "I" come from? "I" is an illusion created by the intellect to give a sense of continuity and security to the human experience. Truly, there is no me.

What is the purpose of life? Education. That is obvious. Life is all learning. If we're learning, we're growing. And if we are growing, we are living. Death is graduation.

What happens when I die? I don't know. This unknown is life's greatest mystery. What I do know is that the only True security is knowing from experience, not from faith or belief, that what I am is consciousness, and consciousness has always been and always will be.

Jordan Lashley will die. Stars will explode, and new ones will form. But consciousness always is. It is without beginning or end. It is the ground of all being. Everything comes out of it and returns to it, like a wave in the ocean.

©2023 Photo by Tara Morris

About the Author

Jordan Lashley is a yoga instructor with eighteen years of experience studying, teaching, and sharing this beautiful practice with students of all levels. He completed his 200-hour RYT training in 2009 at the Baptiste Yoga Studio in Cambridge, MA, and has also completed comprehensive trainings in jivamukti yoga, with Sharon Gannon and David Life, yin yoga with Josh Summers, and a 300-hour yoga philosophy certification from Embodied Philosophy.

His physical and spiritual practice has been shaped and cultivated by many well-loved teachers and mentors. Jordan is also a dedicated mentor to many yoga students and newer teachers as they begin their own teaching journeys.

He believes that yoga is about balance in every possible way. Strength, flexibility, balancing on one foot, balancing your emotional state, your mental perspective, your life... We are at our best when we achieve as much balance as possible.

He is forever grateful to his wife, Angela, for bringing him to the mat all those years ago to discover his own balance. He strives to incorporate all facets of balance into his life, every day, in his favorite role as Dad to daughter Penelopi.

Jordan teaches meditation, breath control, mantra, HOT postural yoga with a powerful dynamic flow, and philosophy in every class.

www.burningwheelyoga.com